RaNDy's FisHMaRKeT ReStaURant

COOKBOOK

Naples, Florida

RANDY'S FISHMARKET RESTAURANT
COOKBOOK

by Randy and Georgianna Essig

Randy Essig
Randy's Fishmarket Restaurant, Inc.
10395 Tamiami Trail N.
Naples, FL 34108
or
email: info@randysfishmarketrestaurant.com

ISBN 978-0-9796616-0-0

Printed in Singapore
CS Graphics
CS Graphics is on the leading edge of
environmentally-safe printing in Asia,
with its solvent and dampening fluid recycling
and energy-efficient press cooling system.

First Edition

Dedicated to our fathers, John R. Essig IV and Isaac Newton, and our mothers, Kathryn and Shirley. Many thanks for the words of wisdom, business acumen, experience, and guidance. Most of all, thanks for your unwavering support through thick and thin.

Special thanks to my mother, Kathyrn, through whose fingers passed innumerable Rosary beads worrying about me!

Love,
Randy and Georgi

Keep on Cookin!!!
Randy

SPECIAL THANKS

BOOK AND COVER JACKET DESIGN

Susan Caldwell

S Caldwell Design, Santa Fe, New Mexico

FOOD PHOTOGRAPHY

Vanessa Rogers Photography, Naples, Florida

www.vanessarogers.com

FOOD STYLING / RECIPE AND INTRO WRITING AND EDITING

Michael di Beneditto

www.michaeldibeneditto.com

CHEF OF RECORD

Chef Ross Peterson, Naples, Florida

PROJECT DEVELOPMENT

Randy and Georgianna Essig

EDITORIAL WORK

Steven Hackett

PHOTOGRAPHY & FOOD STYLING ON PAGES

40, 45, 61, 65, 81, 86, 95, 128-129, 133, 134, 186, 188 AND 191

Robb Stan, G&R Media Services, Naples, Florida

DESSERT RECIPE DEVELOPMENT ON PAGES 170, 173, 178, 189 AND 193

George Smith

WINE PAIRINGS

Colleen Foster

Many thanks to RobinJill Hochmeyer at Doubletree Guest Suites
Naples, Florida 239.593.8733 www.DoubletreeNaples.com

Historic Naples Photos courtesy of Collier County Museum, Naples, Florida
Contemporary Naples Photos Compliments of the Naples Marco Island
Everglades Convention and Visitors Bureau
Waterfront Photos Courtesy of JoNell Modys

...and last, but not least, many thanks to the Staff of Randy's Fishmarket Restaurant
for their patience and assistance during the photo shoot!

FOREWORD

WHEN I HEARD RANDY ESSIG was writing a cookbook, I was delighted. I've eaten at Randy's Fishmarket Restaurant on numerous occasions – and previously up the road at Rodes, which he helped launch – and always enjoyed excellent meals.

"Finally," I remember thinking after my initial dining experience, "I've found someone in Southwest Florida who knows seafood and how to cook it."

As a professional food writer and restaurant reviewer who moved here from the Chesapeake Bay area of Maryland a dozen years ago, I quickly become frustrated by the lack of properly prepared treasures from the sea.

I was used to the best of the best. But then as now, many local kitchens were into overkill, smothering delicate fish with heavy beurre blanc sauces, even adding oddities such as citrus pesto. And what they frequently do to sweet, tender crab meat is downright criminal.

But Randy always gets it right. Try his simple – and simply delicious – soft shell crab preparation and you'll see what I mean.

Randy knows desserts, too. After sampling one of his awesome seafood dinners, be sure to dig into a slice of his Key Lime Pie, once one of Naples' best-kept secrets but now known throughout the nation.

In September 2005, Randy made his debut touting those cool, creamy pies on QVC, a home shopping network that boasts approximately 87 million viewers.

QVC operators took 810 orders as a result of the eight minute, 23 second spot. As the saying goes, the rest is history. Randy now regularly appears on QVC.

In his easy-to-navigate cookbook, you'll see how simple it is to make this stellar Key lime pie yourself. But most of all, you'll learn that you don't need a culinary school degree – or fancy ingredients – to be a first-rate seafood cook.

By L.G. Gordon, Naples Daily News, Food Critic

CONTENTS

IT IS WITH GREAT PLEASURE that I welcome you to Randy's Fishmarket Restaurant Cookbook. I believe that at our establishment, we set the standard for fresh seafood in Southwest Florida. Whether you're stopping by to pick up some fresh seafood from our market or if you're having a seat in the dining room to order something from the menu, you can be assured that you will be getting the freshest seafood possible.

There's an old Polish proverb that says, "Fish, to taste right, must swim three times – in water, in butter and in wine." I only wish to add that, in my humble opinion, the fish should do all three things on the same day! I only select the best of the day's catch for my market and restaurant...local fish, fresh and preservative-free.

Same thing goes for everything else we use in the restaurant. For example, our salad greens are organic. Most of our vegetables and produce are purchased from local growers whenever possible.

If cooking is an art, you don't really have to be the equivalent of a Rembrandt or a Picasso to impress your friends and family. Best of all, you'll have fun doing it! Successful cooking doesn't rely on complicated recipes and exotic ingredients. Simplicity is best. All you need is patience, an unhurried approach, and most important of all... fresh ingredients. Use fresh herbs whenever possible. They taste great and they add color to your dishes. When a recipe calls for lemon juice, squeeze one! Don't pour it from a bottle! And always remember that there's a big difference between shopping for beef and for seafood...an aged steak is great, aged seafood isn't! Fish should smell like the ocean...if it smells like fish, it's too late!

As famed New York critic Harriet van Horne once said, "Cooking is like love, it should be entered into with abandon or not at all!" This is my approach, and it should be yours. So if you've already done your shopping, pour yourself a glass of wine and let's get cooking and have some fun! Or stop by the restaurant...I'll do the cooking, my incredible staff will take good care of you, and we'll all have lots of fun together!

Randy Essig

There is an Irish proverb that says, "Laughter is brightest where food is best." Nowhere in the world will you appreciate these words more than at Randy's Fishmarket Restaurant, where expert chefs will entice you with the best seafood, the dedicated staff will tend to your every need, and the owner's friendly demeanor and off-beat sense of humor will fill your visit with laughter.

"When I was a kid growing up in Syracuse, my first job was frying fish on Friday nights at a local seafood market. Wow, we sold a lot of fish on Friday! Times were different back then... all our Catholic customers believed they had to eat fish on Friday so they wouldn't wake up in hell on Saturday!"

"Not long after I started, my boss asked why I didn't go out after work like all the other kids. He said I should be hanging around with my friends or dating my girl, but I told him I smelled so much like fish from working that darn fryer all night that I couldn't get a date with a new Corvette and fifty-dollar bill!"

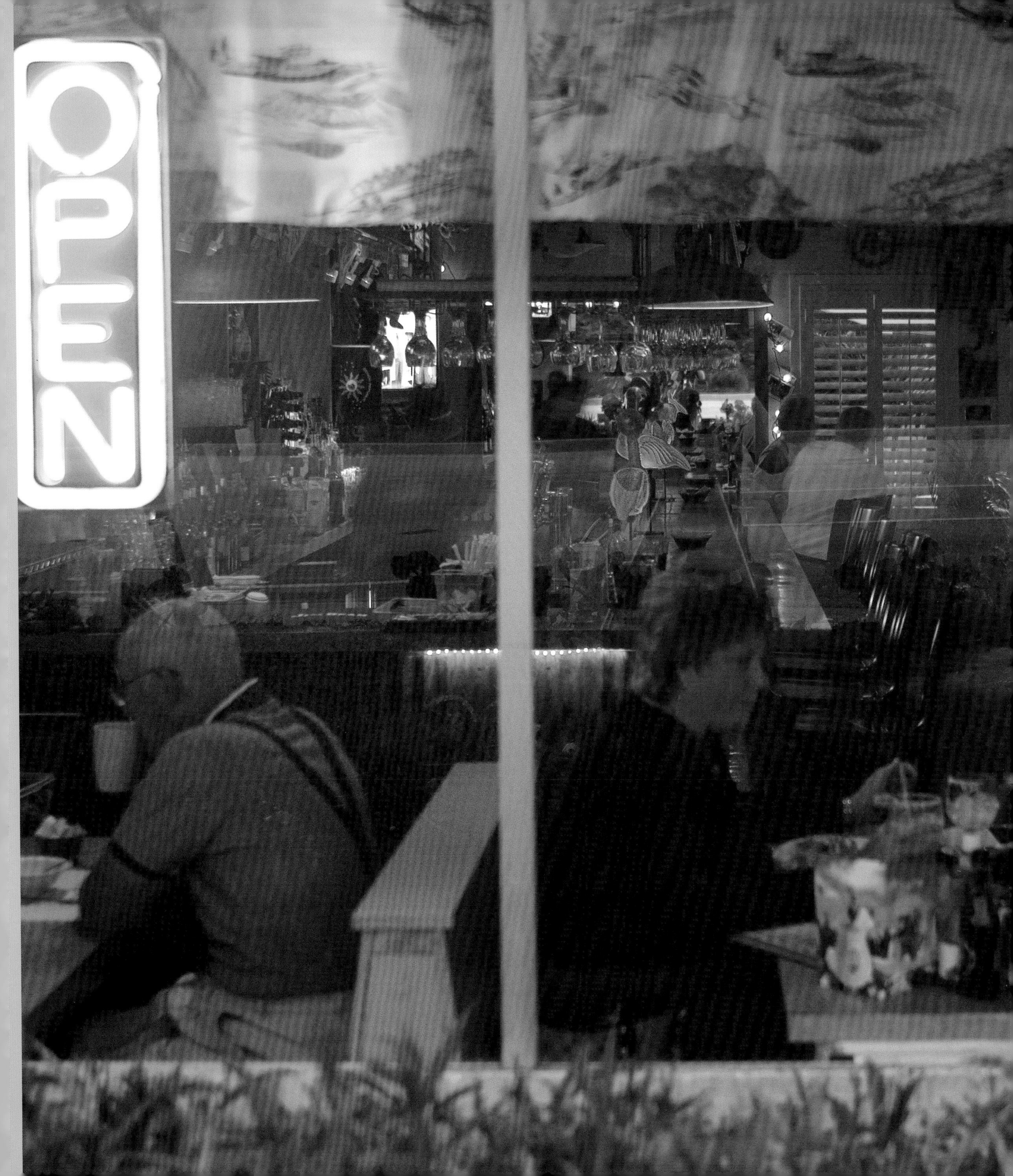
OPEN

Randy Essig knew that his future was in the food business from the time he started working in the fish market while still in junior high school, and he has come a long way since that first job. He was in the nightclub business for many years, but his club was just a career stop-over on his way to greater things in the food business.

"The nightclub business was fun, but my heart was really in the food business," Randy explains.

Randy and his wife, Georgianna, were vacationing in the winter of 1978 when they happened across a true local specialty, Key Lime Pie, in a little restaurant in Port Orange, Florida.

"The waitress suggested it for dessert. I had never even heard of Key Lime Pie, but it looked so good we just couldn't resist. It was the best pie I'd ever eaten."

It wasn't long after the Florida vacation that the Essigs decided they had had it with New York winters. The South was calling! While still retaining some of their business interests in New York, they moved to Naples, Florida, and Randy began his search for his next opportunity in the food business. In 1989, he and a partner bought a local produce market that had plenty of room for expansion. A fish market, a restaurant and a gourmet food department were soon added.

Remembering that terrific dessert from the 1978 vacation, Randy spent years creating his version of the perfect Key Lime Pie. The acquisition and expansion of the produce market finally gave him an outlet for the finished product, Randy's Famous Key Lime Pie.

Randy and his original partner in the produce market parted ways in the late 1990's. Randy was on to bigger and better things. In 1999 he spotted a great location for his current venture, Randy's Fishmarket Restaurant. He contacted the property owners, Lee Bowein and her son, Lloyd Bowein, a local attorney with a sharp eye for a good investment. Lee and Lloyd were well aware of Randy's superb reputation as a restaurateur, and they told Randy that they would readily agree to a deal… with one condition: The Boweins wanted to be partners in the new venture. (*Who said attorneys didn't know much about business?*)

Randy and the Boweins struck a deal, construction soon commenced, and on September 2, 2003, after two-and-a-half years of construction and expert decorating by Randy's wife, Georgianna, Randy's Fishmarket Restaurant finally opened for business. Randy had no problem staffing up…many long-time employees from Randy's previous venture were lined up to work for the celebrated restaurateur. And even though September is traditionally the slowest month of the year in Naples, it was standing room only from the first day at Randy's.

"We've been open a little over three years, and we couldn't be happier about the positive response we've had from the community and from the customers who visit us from all across the U.S., Europe and South America," says Randy.

"We've got exactly the type of restaurant I envisioned before we started this venture…a casual, laid back, family-oriented Key West-style fish house. A few of the 'five-o'clock regulars' in the Tap Room casually mingle with first-time customers and repeat visitors. In the dining room, you'll see everyone from nervous young couples on their first date to three generations of a family laughing it up at a big table.

Look around the room and you are as likely to see one of the world's top golfers or a movie star as you are to see a couple of local business people having lunch. It's the type of place where people come in the first time as customers and return again and again as friends."

"My name is on the front of the building, but it's my staff's dedication to top-notch service and great food that makes this place the hit that it is today. I want to thank Lee and Lloyd Bowein, and the staff that makes Randy's Fishmarket Restaurant successful."

Georgianna Essig

Georgianna Essig shares husband Randy's love of the food business. In the past she has owned and operated two popular gourmet food shops in Marco Island and Naples, Florida. Working behind the scenes as a baker, Georgianna also developed the recipes for some of the restaurant's scrumptious baked goods, most notably the banana bread and best-selling Key Lime Cakes (page 185).

Georgianna's creativity extends far beyond the kitchen. The walls of her Santa Fe and Naples studios, where she works as a pastel artist, are covered with degrees and certifications in art history and art restoration from Ohio State University and the Art Restoration Institute in New York City. Georgianna's most high-profile work, though, is her outstanding interior/exterior design work on Randy's

first Florida restaurant, and most recently on Randy's Fishmarket Restaurant.

Anyone who knows the Essigs knows that their success has been a collaborative effort going back over forty years. Georgianna and Randy met in 1966 while still in high school, and they were married eleven years later in 1977. Ah! Blissful romantics they are!

A Special Thanks

TO LURLINE S. BOWEIN

Thank you for your shining example and endless patience. But most of all your belief that all things are possible through hard work, discipline and perseverance.

Lee lived life with an extraordinary passion that she shared to help transform and inspire many lives. It is this vision and support that was instrumental in the success of Randy's Fishmarket Restaurant, now a landmark restaurant in Naples, Florida. A special place will always be set for her at our table.

From left to right: Lloyd Bowein, Randy Essig, Lee Bowein and Robert 'Bo the Pie Man' Barclay

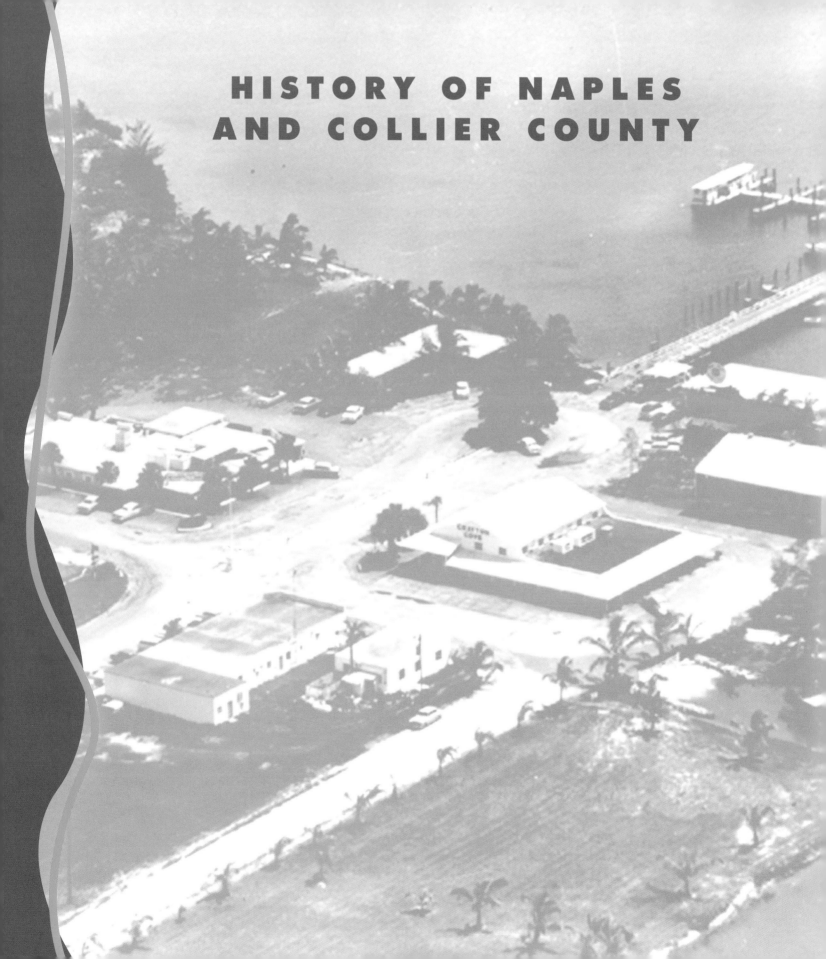

HISTORY OF NAPLES AND COLLIER COUNTY

FOR MILLIONS OF YEARS THE WAVES WASHED upon the sun drenched white sugar sand of Southwest Florida. The Calusa Indians knew the beauty and easy living that awaited those that would make these beaches home, but after the Calusa were driven from these shores by disease and the guns of early Spanish explorers, the land lay empty.

In the late 1800's the U.S. survey teams were surveying the Southwest coast of Florida and reporting back to the senate what a beautiful place Southwest Florida could be. Throughout the 1870's and '80's, magazine and newspaper stories telling of the area's mild climate and abundant fish and game likened it to the sunny Italian peninsula. The name Naples caught on when promoters described the bay as "surpassing the bay in Naples, Italy."

In 1885 two of Naples' earliest settlers, Walter Haldeman and General John S. Williams, bought land and in a few years were running the Naples Town Improvement Company. In the next few years both Williams and Haldeman built homes on the beach, hired a Fort Myers firm to build a pier and had survey teams plan their city. One of the first improvements Haldeman and the Naples Company made was to build a pier 600 feet into the Gulf of Mexico. The unusual "T" shape allowed large ships to dock easily. Despite being destroyed and rebuilt three times, the pier's "T" shape remains.

At the center of their city was the sixteen-room Naples Hotel. They located their hotel two blocks inland from the pier at the narrowest piece of land between the beach and the bay. The hotel opened in 1889, and Rose Cleveland, the sister of President Cleveland, was the first guest.

In 1911, Barron G. Collier, who had made his fortune in streetcar advertising, visited nearby Useppa Island. He was so taken with the area that he bought over a million acres of untouched swampland – including most of Naples. Collier believed that Florida's west coast could enjoy the same boom that the east coast was experiencing in the 1920's; but first it was necessary to bring in roads and railroads.

Based on Collier's promise to help build the Tamiami Trail, in 1923 the state legislature created Collier County, of which Naples is the county seat. Collier spent more than $1 million of his own money to construct the Tamiami Trail, which opened in 1926 as the only paved highway linking the state's two largest cities – Tampa and Miami.

Naples quickly gained a reputation as a winter resort. Social life revolved around the Naples Hotel, which played host to celebrities such as Rose Cleveland, Thomas Edison, Harvey Firestone, Greta Garbo, Hedy Lamarr, and Gary Cooper. As the town of Naples went up, so did the price of property. The cost of a beachfront lot soon reached a whopping $125. Today, that same lot could easily fetch $8 million or more!

Baron Collier died before he could see his dream come true, but come true it did. Today, Naples enjoys unparalleled prosperity. And the area's unrivaled golfing, sport fishing, hunting, boating, sun bathing, and beach combing attract people today just as it did a century ago.

Another early Naples visionary, Ed Crayton, came to town in 1912 or 1913 from St. Petersburg where he had been successful as a land developer. He met a woman who was working for Walter Haldeman's son, General Haldeman, as a general secretary. They fell in love and were soon married. At the same time, Mr. Crayton bought all of Haldeman's property except for his home. Thus a new chapter in Naples history was started. Mr. Crayton worked on Naples development until his death in 1938, at which time his property passed to Mrs. Lindsey Crayton.

The first bank in Collier County was built in 1923 in Everglades City. It was 26 years before Mamie Tooke, often called the Mother of Naples, opened the first bank in Naples in 1949 on Fifth Avenue South. In 1989, it became Barnett Bank.

In 1923, the Frank family lived upstairs over the Ed Frank Garage near 10th Street South. This was the first commercial building on Fifth Avenue South. Mrs. Frank would throw her table scraps to alligators in the swamp below which eventually was filled in with old cars and motors. This family was one of the first settlers in the area. They are noted for having opened the first car dealership. Mr. Frank invented the first swamp buggy and also built the first strip mall.

The Naples Depot began providing train service on January 7, 1927. The last train to leave Naples was in 1971 when the service was discontinued. The Depot has since been restored and is today used by many community organizations for functions. A train whistle is blown at noon every day – just as it was in the early days of Naples.

NAPLES TODAY...

In the short span of thirty years, the number of County residents swelled from 6,488 in 1950, to a phenomenal 85,000 by 1980. The County seat was transferred from Everglades City to East Naples in 1962, and signaled a new era of sustained growth in agriculture, tourism, and real estate that have made Collier County one of the fastest developing areas in the nation. As of July 1, 2005 the population of Collier County stood at 307,000!

Life's a beach

The splendor of Naples begins with its powdery white sand beaches, which extend from the recreational settings of the parks and public access beaches near downtown Naples to the more secluded seaside havens to the north. Naples' beaches are regarded among the finest in the world, and offer visitors a tranquil and beautiful escape from everyday life.

Take a stroll

Naples is also perhaps one of the best places in Florida for a scenic stroll. Opportunities for relaxing walks are plentiful in Naples, as beautiful architecture meets wondrous window shopping and trendy cafés. Secluded courtyards, outdoor sculptures and beautiful fountains highlight historic buildings throughout downtown Naples. The Naples Historical Society offers guided walking tours downtown beginning from the historic Palm Cottage on 12th Street near Naples Pier.

NAPLES HOTEL
NAPLES, FLA.

Family Fun

More families are discovering the delights of Naples. Naples Zoo at Caribbean Gardens is fully accredited by the American Zoo & Aquarium Association, and offers unique shows and interactive animal experiences including the "Meet the Keeper" series, the multimedia "Planet Predator" show and a boat ride to tour the zoo's cage free primate islands within a large lake.

Golf Capital

With nearly 90 golf courses in the Greater Naples area, the region is frequently either first or second in USA rankings of most golf holes per capita. A growing number of public courses provide ample opportunity for visitors to get into the swing. However, many area resorts either own their own private courses or have affiliate relationships with area private clubs.

Unparalled Shopping

In historic shopping districts and waterfront plazas, Naples visitors can find unique treasures ranging from original artwork by the masters to designer fashions. Third Street South, Naples' business district at the turn of the century, now serves as a premier shopping and dining district.

Just a few blocks away, Fifth Avenue South has undergone a renaissance. Famed architect and urban planner Andres Duany leads the innovative redesign effort ten years ago that has transformed Fifth Avenue South into a dynamic pedestrian-friendly scene both day and night.

A short walk from Fifth Avenue South is historic Tin City. Located at a waterfront dockside boardwalk, the eclectic tin-roofed shopping and entertainment venue features nautical and nature-themed gift shops and casual seafood restaurants on the water. Across the street you'll find Bayfront, Naples' newest shopping, dining and entertainment center.

The waterfront Village on Venetian Bay, evocative of the townhouses of Venice, is a destination for sophisticated fashion, jewelry, gourmet shops and fine dining in a picturesque environment.

Nearby at the Waterside Shops at Pelican Bay, you'll find boutiques, shops and restaurants surrounded by lush landscaping, covered walkways and sparkling waterways. Saks Fifth Avenue anchors numerous elegant specialty shops, with an impressive list of luxury shops including Tiffany & Co. and Cartier.

Coastland Center, the regional mall in Naples, encompasses 950,000 square feet of enclosed climate-controlled shopping, including 150 stores and small specialty shops. Prime Outlets is a haven for those with an eye for value.

Dining

Naples has arrived on the culinary map. Fresh seafood, including local stone crab claws caught in season between October and May, are available at Naples favorite seafood restaurant, Randy's Fishmarket Restaurant!

Chef Robin Haas of Miami opened his signature Baleen restaurant overlooking the Gulf at the LaPlaya Beach & Golf Resort, and diners seeking the very finest cuisine have the option of dining in five-diamond style at Artisans in The Dining Room at The Ritz-Carlton, Naples. Chef Tony Ridgway displays Southwest Florida inspired innovation with classic touches at his Ridgway Bar and Grill in Old Naples.

Arts and culture

Culture abounds in Naples. From theatre to dance, to its 134 art galleries and numerous fascinating museums, greater Naples is recognized internationally as a destination for the culturally minded. Naples was named the #1 Small Art Town in America in 2005 by author and art critic Robert Villani. The Naples Museum of Art houses 15 galleries with both permanent and traveling exhibits. The Philharmonic Center for the Arts brings the finest in music, theatre and dance to Naples each season. Naples Dinner Theatre provides professional productions of Broadway favorites year round. The Naples Players perform at downtown Naples' Sugden Theater. Historical museums abound, featuring information on the area's early inhabitants, the Calusa Indians, as well as early Southwest Florida pioneers.

Spas

Relaxation is a way of life in Naples, and an abundance of spas now serve the area. Some of the newest are The Spa on Fifth at The Inn on Fifth, Spa Terre at the LaPlaya Beach & Golf Resort, the Spa at The Naples Beach Hotel & Golf Club and The Spa at The Ritz-Carlton, Naples.

Accomodations

From life at the top to accommodations for the budget-minded, Naples has an excellent array of hotels, motels and resorts. Newer properties include Bellasera, The Ritz-Carlton Golf Resort, Naples – one of two Ritz-Carlton resorts in the city, and the LaPlaya Beach & Golf Resort. Newly renovated properties include Bayfront Inn on Fifth, Naples Grande Resort & Club, Edgewater Beach Hotel & Club, Quality Inn & Suites Park-shore, the Lemon Tree Inn, The Inn on Fifth and The Naples Beach Hotel & Golf Club. For a full listing of area accommodations and direct online booking, visit Collier County's official visitor information site, www.paradisecoast.com.

On the water

Whether it's a sunset cruise aboard the Naples Princess yacht or the Lady Stirling schooner, a nature cruise on the Gordon or Cocohatchee rivers or a private charter to either the Ten Thousand Islands or the Gulf, there is no shortage of ways to get on the water from Naples.

Back to nature

One of the beauties of Naples is that it is surrounded by thousands of acres of private, state and federally preserved land. Within short driving distance you can be bird watching or adventuring at Corkscrew Swamp Sanctuary, Lake Trafford, Delnor-Wiggins Pass State Park, Collier-Seminole State Park, Big Cypress National Preserve, Fakahatchee Strand Preserve State Park, Picayune Strand State Forest, or Everglades National Park, with an entrance in Everglades City. Right in town you can get back to nature at popular attractions including the Naples Nature Center, Naples Botanical Garden, the Cocohatchee Nature Center and Naples Zoo at Caribbean Gardens.

By Steven Hackett

Birds eyeview -

PLEASE DON'T PARK HERE

FISH, FISH, FISH

I can't stress enough that whenever shopping for ANY type of fish or shellfish, make sure you choose a market that has a high turn-over and let your nose be the judge. If the market has a clean aroma, reminiscent of the salty sea or ocean air, then you're in luck. If it smells as we say, "fishy", then immediately rethink today's menu. But if a seafood recipe IS on the agenda and you can shop at a great market, then the same "nasal" rule applies to seafood. So don't buy questionable fish and do complain if the fish you purchase is not top quality.

Make sure you pack your car with a cooler of ice before venturing out, so that you can transport your purchase safely from market to kitchen. When you get home, immediately remove the seafood from its plastic bag and place it in a bowl if shellfish or on a plate if filets or whole fish, cover very lightly with foil and store in the coldest part of your refrigerator. Don't keep seafood any longer than a day in the frig and if possible, cook the fish within the same day of purchase. If for some reason you're not able to prepare it that day, then seal it in a zip lock bag and freeze at once. Freezing is acceptable but not preferable because it breaks down the protein in fish causing a mushy, watery result. Also the fish will exude much of its natural juices rendering it less flavorful. Never freeze mussels, clams or oysters if they are not shucked.

The following section is a general guideline for information about and visuals for buying fresh seafood.

Clams

Clams can basically be divided into two categories, the soft-shell, though their shells are really not soft but they are brittle and hard-shell clams which do have hard shells. We'll focus on the hard shell variety since we use them in this book.

Hard-clams are harvested year round and are graded and marketed by the depth of the shell at the hinge side or they are immediately shucked and then canned. There are many varieties, such as manila, littleneck and cherrystone which are suited to eating raw or steamed or shucked for use in chowders. Pacific littlenecks are best for steaming or in chowders and are not suited for eating raw. The Florida Quahog, pronounced co' hog, both northern and southern varieties which are one of the largest of clams are perfect for chowders and in fritters which we include in several recipes.

Oysters

Oysters had been cultivated by the Romans over two thousand years ago since the ancient myth is that they believed oysters would increase sexual potency…though this has never been proven. Either way there's no denying that eating raw oysters on the half shell can be sensuous.

Most of the best oysters come from the Atlantic Ocean. They are also harvested in the Pacific but the ones that come from the north are usually more flavorful since oysters like colder waters. Their dark shells are quite hard and take a little practice to open. Oysters are usually served raw on the half shell or in chowders or deep fried.

Live clams or oysters should be free of cracks and should close tightly when tapped. Discard any clams that do not close easily; this is an indication that the shellfish are dead. They will remain alive for up to five days in the refrigerator in a bowl, uncovered. Never place them directly on ice and never immerse them in water for storage purposes. Store shucked clams or oysters for up to five days.

HOW MUCH TO BUY?
In-shell, figure 6 whole clams or oysters per serving. If shucked: $1/2$ pint per serving.

Grouper

Grouper is a member of the sea bass family and is found in tropical and warm temperate waters worldwide. Over 400 species can be found around coral reefs of the coastal shelf. The firm, white-flaked flesh contains no intramuscular structure which makes it virtually boneless. The skin is tough and strongly flavored and should be removed during cleaning or before cooking.

Grouper is sold mostly in filets but sometimes can be found in steak form. It lends itself well to any form of cooking but because it is a lean fish, some basting is necessary while broiling or roasting to keep the flesh moist. The heads are very cartilaginous which produce a rich full-bodied fish stock. The fish should have a firm white and translucent flesh and can be used in this book for any recipes calling for a firm-fleshed white fish. Store as any other filleted fish. See intro.

HOW MUCH TO BUY?
Figure about $1/2$ pound per serving.

Mahi-Mahi

Mahi-mahi also known as dolphinfish or Dorado, is one of the most beautiful fish in the sea, brilliantly colored with an iridescent bluish green and gold body. The mahi-mahi is not the mammal called dolphin nor does it look anything like it…don't worry, you're not eating Flipper! They prefer the warmer tropical and subtropical waters of Hawaii, the Caribbean and Gulf Coast of Florida.

Mahi-mahi is sold as steaks, fillets and loins and is perfect for grilling, broiling or pan-roasting but make sure you remove the skin before cooking which is thick and tough. The fish should have a firm white and translucent flesh without separation and discoloration and can be used in this book for any recipes calling for a firm-fleshed white fish. Store as any other filleted fish. See intro.

HOW MUCH TO BUY?
Figure about $1/2$ pound per serving.

Mussels

Mussels come in many varieties such as the Blue, Green-Lipped, Bay and California, but the Blue mussel is by far the most common in New England and California waters where they grow in the wild and are also cultivated. Blue mussels have very dark blue, smooth shells. California mussels tend to be larger in size and Green-Lipped have an identifiable green edge.

Regardless of which of the mussels you purchase, make sure that they are fresh and alive. Avoid any mussels that are open or have broken or cracked shells which is an indication that they are dead. Sometimes mussels will be open a bit but to tell if they are still alive, tap their shells gently. If they close, they are still alive; if they remain open, do NOT purchase them. Mussels that are light in weight or very heavy should also be avoided. Those that are light may be dead and the heavy ones are most likely full of sand.

Before cooking mussels make sure you remove and discard the beard from each by holding it firmly and yanking it free. Scrub the mussels well with a stiff brush to remove sand and barnacles and soak them for about 10 to 20 minutes in a large bowl covered with cold water to which you've added a tablespoon of flour. This will help them to emit excess sand. Store them as you would shellfish. See intro.

HOW MUCH TO BUY?

Figure about 1 pound per person

Pompano

Pompano can be found in the warm, coastal waters of the Atlantic and Pacific but the best come from South Florida. They are also called sunfish because they can often be spotted flying out of the water and "skipping" across the surface, flashing in the sun. Pompano are considered to be a delicacy because they feed on coquina clams, mole crabs, and other invertebrates which con- tribute to their sweet, flavorful meat. These fish are super flat with silvery green to gray skin.

Pompano is sold either whole or filleted, whole being best for grilling, roasting or deep fried and filets, grilled, broiled, pan-seared or deep fried. The fish should have a firm white and translucent flesh – not opaque, and can be used in this book for any recipes calling for a firm-fleshed white fish. Store as any other filleted fish. See intro.

HOW MUCH TO BUY?

If filets, figure $1/2$ pound per serving. If whole: $1^1/2$ to 2 pound fish for 2 to 3 servings.

Red Snapper

Red Snapper are found off the Gulf and Atlantic Coasts of Florida. They are one of the most commonly desired deep-sea delicacies because of their slightly sweet yet unassertive flavor, which stands for reason since they feed on a variety of bottom dwelling crustaceans and small fishes. The Red Snapper industry began in 1870 in Pensacola, Florida, by an enterprising New Englander and "true red snapper", as they are so labeled, are easily distinguished from other red-colored snappers because they have bright-red eyes and are completely red in color. Red Snapper are sold whole or in filets. If purchased whole, make sure their eyes are bright red and glossy and if in filet form, the lean flesh should be firm and a little pink-tinted. Store as any other filleted fish. See intro.

HOW MUCH TO BUY?

If filets, figure $^1/_2$ pound per serving. If whole: $1^1/_2$ to 2 pound fish for 2 to 3 servings and a $3^1/_2$ to 4 pound fish for 6.

Scallops

Bay or Calico scallop meats vary from creamy white to light tan or pink and measure about $^1/_2$ inch to $^3/_4$ inch in diameter. Sea scallops are larger usually measuring about $1^1/_2$ inches in diameter. Both should have translucent flesh and avoid buying any that are opaque.

HOW MUCH TO BUY?

Figure about $^1/_3$ to $^1/_2$ pound per serving.

Shrimp

Shrimp is the most popular seafood in the United States. Hundreds of species are harvested from freshwater and saltwater. There are four species of commercial value shrimp in the Gulf of Mexico and South Atlantic waters. They are categorized by four major colors:

• Brown shrimp are actually pink shrimp and are found along the Atlantic coast.

• Pink shrimp: those found along the northern Gulf coast are often lemon-yellow and those found in the Florida Tortugas are truly pink and sometimes sold with their heads.

• White shrimp are grayish-white with a green, red or blue tinge on the tail.

• Royal Red shrimp are usually deep red to sometimes grayish pink.

Shrimp are sized and sold by count, which is the number of shrimp per pound, either whole or headless. For example, shrimp sold as 16-20 count means there are 16 to 20 per pound. Counts of shrimp range from the largest, under 10 per pound to 300-500 per pound, the smallest. Shrimp

are available in fresh or frozen forms, although most all shrimp sold as "fresh" have actually been previously frozen since they come from all over the world. Gulf and Florida shrimp which are sold truly fresh, not frozen. The most common form is headless, raw with shell-on and they should have tightly adhering shells and firm flesh. Shrimp are also sold as "Peeled Shrimp" which means that the shell has been removed and they come in a variety forms, including "P.U.D." (peeled undeveined), "P&D" (peeled and deveined) and "Tail-On" (peeled with the tail fin and adjacent shell segment left on). Look for firm, crisp flesh. If buying fresh shrimp, store as you would other shellfish. See intro. If frozen, place them immediately back into the freezer if you do not plan on using them that day. If they happen to be on the day's menu, then place them in a shallow bowl and let them thaw naturally. Do not run them under water to thaw as many supermarkets do – they will absorb more water than they already have making them very difficult to sauté or grill. Drain them and dry thoroughly on paper towels.

HOW MUCH TO BUY?

If raw, headless and unpeeled, figure on $^1/_3$ pound per serving. If peeled and deveined: $^1/_4$ pound per serving.

Stone Crabs

Stone Crabs are found along the Atlantic and Gulf Coasts but are commercially harvested almost entirely in Florida. They differ from all other crabs in that they are harvested only for their oversized claws which makes it possible to harvest them without killing them. Since the stone crabs can regenerate their claws three to four times, Florida law forbids the taking of the whole crab. Fishermen are allowed only to take claws that are a minimum of $2^3/_4$ inches long and are required to return the de-clawed crabs safely to the water.

Stone Crab's claws are distinctly recognizable by their dark black tips and they have an interesting mark on the inside of the claw that resembles a thumb print. Their highly nutritious meat is considered a delicacy resembling lobster in appearance and flavor. It is a Florida law that the claws can only be sold fully cooked, always boiled. They are always cooked immediately after harvest to prevent the meat from sticking to the inside of the shell. Some are sold already cracked but you might have to do this yourself or just ask your fishmonger to crack them for you. They are almost always served ice cold in their shell with a sauce such as a remoulade or just plain and simple with drawn butter. They can be stored as you would shellfish. See Intro.

HOW MUCH TO BUY?

Here's the tricky part! They say to figure on 3 or 4 per person but honestly I could eat a dozen myself, they're so addicting! I'll let you be the judge but I must remind you that they are quite expensive since they're in short supply.

Yellowfin Tuna

Torpedo shaped and beautifully colored, the Yellowfin tuna, also known as "Ahi" is a member of the very large mackerel family making it one of the larger edible fish in the sea with weight upwards of 400 pounds. They are pelagic and restlessly roam the deeper offshore waters of Florida's Gulf and Atlantic Coasts.

Tuna is oily, rich tasting fish and extremely flavorful. It has a red translucent flesh when raw and white opaque flesh when cooked. It is usually sold in steak form and is perfect for grilling, broiling, pan-searing or serving raw. However you prepare tuna, it is best to cook it very quickly on the medium-rare to rare side. If overcooked it becomes very dry and tough. But before cooking, make sure to remove the dark muscle or sinew from the meat which has a more intense "fishy" flavor. Store as you would fish filets. See intro.

HOW MUCH TO BUY?

Figure about $^1/_2$ pound per serving.

The Captain's Tavern

This cookbook, hopefully the first of many, has been years in the making. I don't mean that it took many years to shoot the photos, write the text, and lay out the graphics. I mean that for me, this book is the culmination of years of personal experience and learning. This book is all about seafood… great seafood. I want to pay tribute to a gentleman who, in my opinion, has set the standard for seafood restaurants not only in Florida, but in the United States. I have learned much from him, and I aspire to experience his success and longevity in this business.

Four out of five new restaurants fail within 18 months, so when you meet a man who has successfully owned and operated a landmark establishment, Captain's Tavern, for 35 years (and that's more than forever in the South Florida restaurant business!) in the same location, you can be sure that this is a man who knows his trade. This is a man who is passionate about food. This man is Captain Bill Bowers.

Captain Bill grew up in coastal New England. His love of the sea was inherited… his grandfather was a sea captain. Bill started working on the fish piers of Gloucester, Massachusetts when he was just a young teen back in the early 1940's, and he has been in the seafood business ever since. (Those who know him well like to say that Bill has no blood… salt water and drawn butter run through his veins!) To this very day, the Captain still brings in two truckloads of fresh seafood from Boston every week.

Today, at age 77, Captain Bill and his dear wife of 25 years, Audrey, spend seven days a week running one of the last independently-owned, old-fashion Florida fish houses. Captain's Tavern is a refreshing break from the rest of Miami. The waitresses are old school and friendly. The food is incredible and interesting, without being frilly. There are many fish in the sea, and most of them are on the Captain's menu. All are pristinely fresh and come cooked in a veritable United Nations of styles. Clam chowder is creamy and full of clams. The lobster bisque will make you think you've died and gone to heaven! Pan-fried soft-shell crab is golden, crispy and sea-sweet. Audrey's island influence is unmistakable in dishes such as Jamaican-Style Whole Yellowtail, Conch Chowder, and Conch Fritters. Also noteworthy is the Portuguese Fish Stew.

The signature cheesecake is almost impossible to pass. They serve meat too. "Captain" Bill Bower's philosophy is to give his customers what they want, so he does have a variety of main courses for land-lubbers, including steaks, lamb chops, duck and chicken. But who would be silly enough to order it? You must ask for the wine list. Food & Wine magazine placed Captain's Tavern near the top of its list of "America's 50 Most Amazing Wine Experiences." (As impressive as the Captain's 600-bottle wine list is, it's surprisingly modest prices.) Other rave reviews have been written in the New York Tribune, the Miami Herald, Zagat and many more. The Captain's Tavern has consistently been named among Miami's top-10 restaurants.

The Captain's Tavern is a GREAT seafood place with dock-like décor… a stylish seafaring theme, with dark wood and brick, dim lighting, nautical art and various other nautical antiquities on the walls. Salt-water aquariums are scattered throughout the dining room, offering plenty to look at as you await your feast. (If you have little kids, hope especially hard for a seat near a fish tank… keeps them happy all night.) If you're looking for glitzy South Beach décor, you've come to the wrong place!

This is a true family-style restaurant. It's a full room of happy people enjoying large portions of great food. They're not the people who make the South Beach scene. They range from University of Miami students to grandparents, young and old. Many are families with two or three generations round a big table. Over 95% of the Captain's customers are "locals"… people who know where to go for the best in town.

The family tradition extends to the kitchen, too. Opened in 1971 with just nine employees, the restaurant today employs over 100 people. The Captain says all seven of his kids have worked in the business, and now the grandchildren are starting to show up for work!

I've included a couple of the Captain's favorite recipes in this book. Try them at home, or stop by and see the Captain in Miami. Bring the family.

Thanks again, Captain, for your hospitality, guidance, and your influence through the years.

Randy

The Captain's Salmon Tartare "Stack"

THE VINAIGRETTE:

THE VINAIGRETTE:

2½ Tbs. olive oil

1 Tb. Japanese seasoned rice vinegar (see remarks)

THE TARTARE:

2 lbs. fresh salmon filet, brown flesh removed and boneless, skinless, and finely chopped

4 large shallots, peeled and finely chopped

4 Tbs. capers, rinsed, drained and finely chopped

2 Tbs. finely chopped fresh chives

Juice of 2 lemons

Salt and freshly ground black pepper

THE CUCUMBER RELISH:

2 medium size cucumbers, peeled, seeded and diced

4 Tbs. sweet chili sauce (see remarks)

1 to 2 t. finely minced jalapeno pepper

Pinch of kosher salt

THE ASSEMBLY:

1 medium size red or sweet yellow onion, peeled and cut crosswise into thin slices

1 large ripe red tomato, stemmed and cut crosswise into thin slices

1 large yellow tomato, stemmed and cut crosswise into thin slices

1 ripe avocado, peeled, pitted and cut lengthwise into thin slices

Eel coating sauce (see remarks)

Sriracha hot sauce (see remarks)

Once you have prepped all of the components, the presentation is quite simple. You will need 6 round molds such as metal flan rings but I like to use 3 inch diameter plastic PVC pipe cut into 2½ inch lengths. They are much easier to buy since it takes just one quick trip to your local hardware store.

Start by making the vinaigrette: In a small bowl, combine the oil and vinegar, whisk until blended and reserve.

The tartare: Combine all of the tartare ingredients in a medium size mixing bowl, season with salt and pepper and mix well. Refrigerate until nicely chilled.

The cucumber relish: In another small bowl, combine all of the relish ingredients, season with a pinch of salt and mix well. Set aside.

The assembly: To make the "stacks", place 1 mold (see intro) in the center of 6 individual serving plates. Layer a slice of onion, then red tomato, yellow tomato and avocado. You will need to create a single thin layer of each component to fill the molds and this may require using a couple slices of each. Drizzle with a little of the vinaigrette and fill each mold with some of the salmon tartare. Press the tartare lightly into a flat even layer and carefully lift and remove each mold from the "stacks". Top each "stack" with a couple drops of eel coating and hot sauce. Spoon a little of the relish onto each plate and serve at once.

SERVES 6

The Japanese vinegar, sweet chili sauce, eel coating sauce and Sriracha hot sauce are available in Asian markets.

1 whole red or white snapper,
about 1½ to 2 lbs., scaled
and cleaned

1 t. kosher salt

1 t. freshly ground black pepper

1 t. garlic powder

6 Tbs. cornstarch

1½ qts. vegetable oil for frying,
such as peanut, corn or canola

THE SAUCE:

2 cups sweet chili sauce
(see remarks)

1 cup water

1 cup tamarind pulp or paste
(see remarks)

4 large garlic cloves,
peeled and finely minced

2 Tbs. Thai fish sauce
(see remarks)

GARNISH:

4 scallions,
trimmed and thinly sliced

¼ cup chopped fresh cilantro

2 mini sweet or mild peppers,
stemmed and thinly sliced

The Captain's Crispy Snapper with Sweet and Sour Chili Tamarind Sauce

If you've never had Florida red snapper, then in my opinion you've really never had snapper at all – the Florida red is in a league all it's own. It's such a delicious, incredible tasting fish that none can compare but unfortunately it's not always readily available outside of Florida. With that said, just make sure whatever whole snapper you do buy, which will probably be the white Pacific snapper or New Zealand red, make sure the fish is very fresh: the skin should be glossy and shiny, the gills nice and red and moist, the flesh very firm and the smell should be clean, reminiscent of the salty ocean air.

Start by preparing the snapper: With a very sharp knife, score the fish on each side in 3 places at an angle and down to the backbone. Season with the salt, pepper and garlic powder and coat both sides with the cornstarch.

Heat the oil in a large skillet or sauté pan over medium heat. Carefully add the fish to the oil and cook for about 10 minutes per side or until the fish is nicely browned and opaque throughout.

While the fish is cooking, make the sauce: In a medium size mixing bowl combine all of the sauce ingredients and whisk until well blended. Transfer the mixture to a medium size saucepan, bring to a boil, reduce heat to low and keep warm.

When the fish is done, remove it from the skillet to a double layer of paper towels. Spoon about ½ cup of the sauce on a large warm platter. Top the sauce with the fried snapper and spoon more of the sauce to completely glaze the fish. Garnish with the scallions, cilantro and peppers and serve hot with steamed jasmine or other white rice and an extra bowl of sauce on the side.

SERVES 2 TO 3

The sweet chili sauce, tamarind pulp or paste and the Thai fish sauce are available in Asian markets.

starters

Tomato, Mozzarella and Red Pepper "Carpaccio"

This very simple dish, consisting of basically two components plus a drizzle of vinaigrette, is believed to have originated on the island of Capri. Subsequently, it has gained such enormous popularity here in the states that it can be found on almost every restaurant menu. The success of the salad relies solely on the freshest of ingredients such as true vine-ripened tomatoes and fresh-made mozzarella. And, at Randy's, we like to layer char-roasted red peppers as well, which makes for an interesting addition of texture and flavor.

2 medium size red bell peppers, kept whole

4 large vine-ripened tomatoes, cut crosswise into $1/2$ inch slices

1 ball (12 oz.) fresh made mozzarella, cut crosswise into $1/4$ inch slices

1 recipe Balsamic Vinaigrette, (see recipe page 158)

Kosher salt and coarsely cracked black pepper

GARNISH:

$1/4$ cup fine julienne of fresh basil leaves

Start by roasting the peppers: You may also roast the peppers on either an electric or gas stove. For an electric stove, place the whole peppers directly on the coils of the burner over medium-high heat until the skins of the peppers are blackened and charred on all sides. For a gas stove, pierce the peppers onto the tines of a long fork through the stem end, set over a medium-high flame and char on all sides. In both cases remove from the burner, wrap in damp paper towels and cool completely. When cool enough to handle, peel off the charred skin, core the peppers and remove stems and seeds. Cut the peppers into slices similar in diameter to the mozzarella and set aside.

On a serving platter or individual salad plates, arrange, alternating slices of tomato, mozzarella and roasted pepper. Drizzle with the vinaigrette and sprinkle with salt and pepper. Garnish with the julienne of basil and serve at once with a crusty loaf of peasant bread.

SERVES 8

Our master baker and pastry chef, Pete Moore, makes by hand fresh mozzarella daily for the "Fishmarket". For the photo shoot, Pete especially made his stunning signature "pinwheel" of fresh mozzarella rolled with Parma prosciutto. You may be able to find something very similar in the cheese section of most top quality supermarkets and if you do, substitute the plain mozzarella with this delicious treat!

Chili Pepper Spiked Conch Fritters

Conch, the second best known edible snail, the first being the escargot is particular to the warm waters of the Atlantic and Caribbean which is why conch fritters are one of the most popular appetizers on every restaurant menu in South Florida. Most restaurants here have their own version of these crunchy spicy morsels and thinks theirs are better than the competitor's. Guess what? So do we!

1 large egg

¾ cup half and half

1 cup all-purpose flour

1½ cups conch meat, ground or chopped

1 small onion, peeled and finely diced

½ medium green bell pepper, cored, seeded and finely diced

½ medium red bell pepper, cored, seeded and finely diced

2 large garlic cloves, peeled and finely minced

2 t. Old Bay Seasoning

½ t. freshly ground white pepper

½ t. Kosher salt

½ t. crushed red chili pepper flakes

1 qt. canola oil

1 recipe Fresh Mango, Papaya and Pineapple Relish, (see recipe page 156)

In a medium mixing bowl, combine the egg and half and half and whisk until well blended. Add the flour and whisk until smooth. Add the remaining ingredients except for the canola oil and whisk until just combined. Cover and refrigerate the batter for at least 30 minutes before frying.

In a large pot or cast-iron Dutch oven, heat the oil to 365 degrees on a candy thermometer. Drop the batter by tablespoonfuls into the hot oil, in batches. Fry the fritters until golden brown. Remove with a slotted spoon and transfer to paper towels to drain. Sprinkle with a little additional kosher salt and serve hot accompanied by mango dipping sauce.

SERVES 8

Coconut Crusted Shrimp

From time to time, we used to run our crispy coconut-coated shrimp skewers as a special but the demand was so great for their return each night, we had no choice but to permanently add them to our menu. They have since become one of our best-selling appetizers and as one customer exclaims, "Your coconut shrimp are the best I've ever had and you can never take them off your menu!" No need to worry, they're here to stay.

16 (12 inch long) wooden skewers

3/4 cup coconut milk, available in Oriental markets

16 colossal shrimp, preferably pink Gulf shrimp, about 15 per pound, peeled and deveined with tails left on

3/4 cup unsweetened shredded coconut

1/2 cup Panko (Japanese bread crumbs)

1/2 t. coarse salt

1/2 t. freshly ground white pepper

1 quart peanut oil

1 recipe Spiced Orange Marmalade Dipping Sauce, (see recipe page 151)

Soak the wooden skewers in water for 1 hour before using.

In a shallow bowl, combine the coconut milk and shrimp and set aside to marinate for 1 hour.

Remove the shrimp from the coconut milk and reserve the milk. Thread one shrimp on each skewer from the tail to the head through the middle of each shrimp and return the shrimp to the coconut milk.

In another shallow bowl, combine the shredded coconut, Panko, salt and pepper and crush lightly with back of a spoon and set aside.

Place the oil in a deep casserole and heat between 325 and 350 degrees on a candy thermometer. Remove half of the shrimp skewers from the milk, dip lightly on all sides in the shredded coconut mixture and add to the hot oil. Fry for 3 minutes or until golden brown and transfer to double layers of paper towels. Continue frying the remaining shrimp in the same method and serve 4 hot shrimp skewers per person accompanied by the marmalade dipping sauce.

SERVES 4

Our Shrimp pairs well with McWilliam's Hanwood Estate Chardonnay, Southeast Australia. Taste Profile: green to pale straw. The subtle clove and cashew nut oak accentuates distinctive white peach aromas.

Deep-Fried Hush Puppies with Honey Butter

There are so many legends surrounding these deep-fried cornmeal breads commonly known as hush puppies but my favorite tells of fishermen taking their dogs with them on overnight trips. When the fishermen would batter dip and fry the catch of the day for dinner, the dogs, enticed by the smell would howl and beg for a taste. To calm their pets, the fishermen would then drop leftover spoonfuls of batter into the hot oil and then throw the fritters to the hungry dogs, while saying… get ready… "Hush, puppies!"

THE HONEY BUTTER:

8 Tbs. salted butter, softened

2 Tbs. honey

THE HUSH PUPPIES:

1 cup yellow cornmeal

1/2 cup sifted all-purpose flour

1/2 t. granulated sugar

1/2 t. baking powder

1/4 t. baking soda

1 t. kosher salt

1 large egg

3/4 cup buttermilk

1/2 cup cream style corn

2 1/2 cups canola oil

Start by making the butter: Combine the butter and honey in a small bowl and whisk until well-blended. Do not over mix.

The hush puppies: In a medium size mixing bowl, combine the cornmeal, flour, sugar, baking powder, baking soda and salt and mix well. Set aside.

Combine the egg and buttermilk in a small bowl and whisk until well blended. Add to the bowl containing the dry ingredients and stir until the dry ingredients just disappear; do not over mix. Fold in the cream style corn and reserve.

Heat the oil in a large heavy skillet, preferably cast-iron, to 350 degrees on a candy thermometer. Drop the batter by the tablespoonful into the hot oil and fry for 3 to 3 1/2 minutes or until golden brown. You might have to fry them in batches. Drain the hush puppies on paper towels and serve hot with the whipped honey butter.

MAKES ABOUT 1 1/2 DOZEN

Golden Brown Fried Plantains

Fried plantains, a staple of Caribbean and Central America cuisine and aptly referred to as "the French fries of the tropical world", have become one of our favorites as well. We like to use sweet ripe plantains, deep-fried and simply sprinkled with a little salt which makes for a delicious accompaniment to many of our seafood recipes. Once you taste them, you'll never make French fries again.

1½ cups canola oil

4 firm ripe plantains

3 Tbs. cornstarch

Kosher salt

In a large heavy skillet, heat the oil to 350 to 375 degrees on a candy thermometer.

Peel the plantains, cut in half crosswise and then cut each half lengthwise into 1/8 inch thick slices. Dredge the slices in cornstarch, shaking off the excess. Add them to the hot oil and fry for 4 to 6 minutes, turning once or twice, until golden brown on both sides. The plantains should be crispy on the outside but soft on the inside.

Remove the slices from the oil with a slotted spoon and transfer to paper towels to drain. Sprinkle with a little kosher salt and serve at once.

SERVES 6 TO 8

Gulf Shrimp Fritters

For those of you who are unable to get good South Florida conch in order to prepare our fritter recipe, this variation is made with shrimp, the ever popular shellfish and is equally delicious. Serve the fritters hot right from the fryer, dipped in creamy aioli and accompanied by a frosted mug of ice cold beer.

1 large egg

2/3 cup half and half

1 cup all-purpose flour

1 t. baking powder

3/4 lb. fresh shrimp, preferably pink Gulf shrimp, about 21-25 per pound, peeled, deveined and finely chopped

1 small onion, peeled and finely diced

1/2 medium green bell pepper, cored, seeded and finely diced

2 large garlic cloves, peeled and finely minced

3 medium scallions, finely minced, green part only

1 medium celery stalk, trimmed and finely minced

2 t. Old Bay Seasoning

1 Tb. Crystal hot sauce or other hot sauce

1/2 t. kosher salt

1/2 t. freshly ground white pepper

1 qt. canola oil

1 recipe Pan-Roasted Garlic and Lemon Aioli, (see recipe page 143)

In a medium size mixing bowl, combine the egg and half and half and whisk until well blended. Add the flour and baking powder and whisk until the mixture is smooth and free of lumps.

Fold in the remaining ingredients, except for the oil, until well blended. If the mixture is too loose, add a few more tablespoons of flour. Cover and refrigerate for at least 30 minutes before using.

In a large pot or cast-iron Dutch oven, heat the oil to 365 degrees on a candy thermometer. Drop the batter by tablespoonful into the hot oil, in batches. Fry the fritters until golden brown. Remove with a slotted spoon and transfer to paper towels to drain. Sprinkle with a little additional kosher salt and serve at once accompanied by the aioli.

SERVES 8

Crispy Chicken Wings, Buffalo Style

I know, I know! Like this is what the world is waiting for, another Buffalo chicken wing recipe, right? Wrong! You might see them on every gosh darn restaurant menu from here in South Florida to there in Southern California, but I must say what sets ours apart is our unique sauce recipe. Besides the predictable melted butter and hot sauce combination found on most menus, we perk it up by adding some herbs, extra seasonings and a little tomato juice which make for an addicting, finger-licking glaze.

THE CHICKEN WINGS:

2 to 2^{1}/$_{2}$ lbs. chicken wings, cut in half at joint and tips removed

1 qt. canola oil

1 Tb. kosher salt

1 t. freshly ground white pepper

THE SAUCE:

4 Tbs. unsalted butter

4 Tbs. Crystal hot sauce or other hot sauce

2 Tbs. tomato juice, preferably Sacramento

1 t. garlic powder

1 t. cayenne pepper

^{1}/$_{2}$ t. chili powder

^{1}/$_{2}$ t. dried thyme

1 t. white vinegar

ACCOMPANIMENT:

1 cup Randy's Blue Cheese Dressing, (see recipe page 159)

3 large celery stalks, trimmed and cut into 4 inch sticks

Start by making the chicken wings: Preheat the oven to 250 degrees. Wrap the wings in paper towels to dry thoroughly and set aside.

In a large deep, heavy skillet heat the oil to 375 to 400 degrees on a candy thermometer. Remove the wings from the paper towels, sprinkle with the salt and pepper and add half of the wings to the hot oil. Fry the wings, turning often, for about 12 to 15 minutes or until they are nicely browned and cooked through. Remove the wings with a slotted spoon to paper towels to drain. Place the wings on baking sheet and keep warm in the preheated oven until the second batch is ready. Continue frying the second batch of wings in the same manner.

Just before the second batch of wings is done, prepare the sauce: Melt the butter in a small saucepan over medium-low heat, whisk in the remaining sauce ingredients and just heat through, about 3 to 4 minutes; do not let the sauce come to boil.

Transfer the sauce to a large mixing bowl, add all of the wings and toss well to coat evenly with the hot sauce. Serve hot with Randy's Blue Cheese Dressing, celery sticks and plenty of napkins!

SERVES 4 TO 5

Half-Moon Seafood Quesadillas

Most quesadillas are prepared like sandwiches where one tortilla is spread with a filling and then topped with another tortilla but ours are quite special since we fill only one tortilla and fold it in half to form a "turnover". You don't have to be locked into any one recipe since quesadillas are quite versatile and can be filled with many different ingredients, especially leftovers you might have on hand, such as steamed vegetables, grilled fish or roast chicken. Let's see your creative side!

2 Tbs. unsalted butter

3 Tbs. finely minced red bell pepper

3 Tbs. finely minced green bell pepper

3 Tbs. finely minced red onion

12 large shrimp, preferably pink Gulf shrimp, about 21 to 25, peeled, deveined and cut into small pieces

10 large sea scallops, cut into small pieces

1 t. garlic powder

1 1/2 t. Crystal hot sauce or other hot sauce

Kosher salt and coarsely cracked black pepper

6 (12-inch) flour tortillas

1 cup shredded cheddar cheese

1 cup shredded Asiago cheese

ACCOMPANIMENT:

Roasted Tomato Salsa, (see recipe page 152)

Florida Avocado Guacamole, (see recipe page 150)

Sour cream

In a 10 inch skillet, melt the butter over medium-high heat. Add the red and green peppers and onions and cook for 2 to 3 minutes or until soft but not browned. Add the shrimp, scallops, garlic and hot sauce and continue cooking for another 2 to 3 minutes, stirring often or until the shellfish turns opaque. Remove the skillet from the heat, season the mixture with salt and pepper and set aside.

Preheat the oven to 250 degrees.

You will be making 6 quesadillas. For each quesadilla: Lay the tortillas flat on a work surface. Divide the seafood mixture evenly and spoon onto one side of each tortilla. Spread the mixture to cover 1/2 of the surface. Sprinkle each portion with some of the cheddar and Asiago cheeses and fold the tortillas in half, covering the seafood mixture completely to create half moon shapes.

Heat a large non-stick skillet over medium-low heat. Place two tortillas at a time in the skillet and cook for 1 to 2 minutes on each side or until the tortillas are spotted brown and the cheeses have melted. Transfer the quesadillas to a cookie sheet and keep warm in the center of the preheated oven. Continue cooking the remaining tortillas in the same manner. Serve hot, cut into wedges with bowls of salsa, guacamole and sour cream.

SERVES 6

drinks

Randy's 'Rita

We love adding salt to the rim of our glasses for Randy's 'Rita, combining both sweet and savory tastes and it's so easy to do. Before pouring the drink into the glass, simply rub a lime wedge around the glass rim and then dip into a small plate of kosher salt. Serve the 'Rita with ice or strained, but either way, make sure it's nice and cold!

3 Tbs. (1½ oz.) tequila

1 Tb. (½ oz.) triple sec or other orange liqueur

6 Tbs. (3 oz.) Margarita mix or sour mix

1 Tb. (½ oz.) freshly squeezed lime juice

Splash of freshly squeezed orange juice

1 Margarita or Martini glass with salted rim (see intro)

1 fresh lime wedge

In a cocktail shaker, combine the tequila, triple sec, Margarita mix, lime juice and orange juice. Add ice, cover and shake vigorously.

Pour the 'Rita into the salted glass and garnish with a lime wedge. Serve at once.

MAKES ONE DRINK

The "Oh My God" Bloody Mary

Besides garnishing our Bloody Mary with the predictable celery stalk and typical lemon or lime wedge, we add to the rim of the glass a perfectly cooked pink colossal Gulf shrimp that we call "Oh My God" for its enormous size. It makes for quite an impressive presentation that's both unique and so delicious.

3 Tbs. (1½ oz.) vodka

8 Tbs. (4 oz.) Whisky Creek Bloody Mary mix or your favorite Bloody Mary mix

Ice

1 celery stalk with leaves

1 fresh lemon or lime wedge

1 cooked colossal shrimp, preferably pink Gulf shrimp, about 15 per pound, peeled and deveined with tail left on

Fill a 12 ounce glass with ice. Add the vodka and Bloody Mary mix and transfer the mixture to a cocktail shaker. Cover and shake vigorously.

Pour the Blood Mary back into the glass. Add the stalk of celery and garnish the rim of the glass with a lemon or lime wedge and the cooked shrimp. Serve immediately.

MAKES ONE DRINK

The Classic Mojito

In this recipe, we call for a Simple Syrup, as many sweet drinks do and as the name suggests, it is quite easy to make. Combine equal parts water and granulated sugar in a small saucepan over medium heat and bring to a boil, stirring constantly, to dissolve the sugar completely. Remove the saucepan from the heat, transfer the syrup to a bowl and let cool. The syrup can then be stored in your refrigerator in an airtight container, forever. With the addition of a little orange liqueur, rum, vanilla or other flavoring, the syrup can be used in a variety of ways, especially for soaking cakes (see Sweet and Tart Key Lime Cake, page 185), poaching fruit or to sweeten fruit sauces. For an interesting variation on our Tres Leches (Three Milk Cake on page 193), soak the plain warm cake with some simple syrup flavored with rum, instead of the milk mixture. Let the cake sit to absorb all of the syrup and serve with a dollop of whipped cream and a mixture of fresh berries.

3 fresh sprigs of mint

6 Tbs. (3 oz.) simple syrup (see intro)

3 Tbs. (1½ oz.) freshly squeezed lime juice

3 Tbs. (1½ oz.) rum

Ice

1 to 2 Tbs. club soda

In a 12 ounce glass, combine 2 sprigs of mint together with the simple syrup and crush or "muddle" the mint with the back of a spoon. Add the lime juice, rum and fill 3/4 of the glass with ice. Transfer the mixture to a cocktail shaker, cover and shake vigorously.

Pour the Mojito back into the glass, top with club soda and serve at once garnished with the remaining sprig of mint.

MAKES ONE DRINK

soups & salads

Cracked Peppercorn and Sesame Crusted Ahi Tuna with a Balsamic Vinaigrette

In our recipes calling for tuna, we like to use Ahi which is yellowfin tuna and to complicate matters further, we specify "sushi grade" but simply put this means that the fish is good enough to eat raw and can be sold for use as rare steaks and sushi. The grade has nothing to do with freshness but only taste, so when asking for "sushi grade" or any other grade of tuna, make sure that the fish you're buying is very fresh, preferably from a reputable fishmonger… or better yet from our own "Fishmarket" here at Randy's!

THE VINAIGRETTE:

1 small garlic clove, peeled and finely minced

1 small shallot, peeled and finely minced

1/2 cup honey

6 Tbs. good quality balsamic vinegar

2 Tbs. finely julienned fresh basil

Kosher salt and freshly ground black pepper

THE TUNA:

2 Tbs. mixed coarsely cracked white and black peppercorns

1 Tb. toasted sesame seeds

1 t. kosher salt

12 oz. fresh Ahi "sushi grade" tuna filet, in one piece

1 1/2 Tbs. canola oil

THE ASSEMBLY:

8 cups mixed field greens, cleaned and well dried

Optional: 2 Florida navel oranges, peeled and cut into segments

Start by making the vinaigrette: In a small bowl combine the garlic, shallot, honey, vinegar and basil and whisk until well blended. Season with salt and pepper and set aside at room temperature.

The tuna and final assembly: Place the lettuces in a large mixing bowl and reserve.

Combine the peppercorns, sesame seeds and salt in a shallow plate. Coat one side of the tuna with the peppercorn mixture and set aside. Heat the oil in a large non-stick skillet over medium-high heat. Add the tuna and quickly sear for 30 seconds on each side keeping the fish rare in the center. Do not overcook. Transfer the filet to a cutting board, cool slightly and then cut crosswise into 1/4 inch slices.

Toss the lettuces with 2/3 of the vinaigrette and divide the salad among 4 individual serving plates. Top each portion with some of the sliced tuna and drizzle with the remaining vinaigrette. Garnish with the optional orange segments and serve at once with a crusty warm baguette.

SERVES 4

The peppercorn seared tuna is so versatile, use sliced and toss into a pasta primavera, fold into a lemon risotto or simply serve on a bed of our flavorful Island Rice Pilaf, see recipe (page 163), accompany with wasabi and soy sauce. If using wasabi powder, reconstitute it by adding 3 tablespoons of it with 1 1/2 tablespoons warm water in a small bowl to form a smooth paste.

Lemon-Scented Shrimp Salad

To cook shrimp perfectly for use in cold preparations such as salads and cocktails, it doesn't matter what size shrimp you are using, the rule of thumb remains the same: bring plenty of lightly salted water to a boil, add the shrimp and just when the water returns to a boil, drain the shrimp immediately. They are now fully cooked yet not overcooked. The larger the shrimp, the longer it will take the water to return to the boil, but don't be concerned, this method works every time.

1 cup mayonnaise

2 Tbs. freshly squeezed lemon juice

1 Tb. Worcestershire sauce

1 t. Old Bay Seasoning

Kosher salt and freshly ground white pepper

4 medium celery stalks, trimmed and sliced

2½ lbs. medium shrimp, preferably pink Gulf shrimp, about 31- 40 per lb., peeled and deveined

½ t. garlic powder

In a large bowl combine the mayonnaise, lemon juice, Worcestershire sauce and Old Bay, season with salt and pepper and whisk until well blended.

Bring 2 quarts of water to a boil, together with the garlic powder and salt to taste, in a large pot. Add the shrimp and cook for about 2 minutes or until they just turn pink. Do not overcook; the shrimp might be done before the water returns to a boil.

Drain the shrimp thoroughly and dry well on double layers of paper towels. While still warm, cut the shrimp into ⅓ inch pieces and add the shrimp to the bowl with the mayonnaise. Taste and correct the seasoning, cover and refrigerate the salad for at least 30 minutes before serving.

Serve the salad chilled on a bed of tender field greens.

SERVES 6

For a more elaborate presentation, fill tomato shells with the salad: Cut off about ½ inch of the tops of medium sized vine-ripened tomatoes and set the tops aside. Hollow out the tomatoes, discarding the pulp and seeds and fill each with some of the shrimp salad. Place the tops back onto the tomatoes, a bit askew. Garnish each with a sprig of fresh Italian parsley and serve chilled.

Mixed Shellfish Salad with a Lemon/Lime Vinaigrette

This simple seafood salad, dressed in a citrus vinaigrette is both light and refreshing and makes for a perfect luncheon dish served well-chilled on a warm summer day. The combination of both tender bay scallops and Gulf shrimp give the salad an interesting texture and flavor.

1 lb. large shrimp, preferably pink Gulf shrimp, about 21 to 25 per lb., peeled, deveined and cut in half

Kosher salt

1 lb. bay scallops

3 Tbs. freshly squeezed lemon juice

3 Tbs. freshly squeezed lime juice

3 Tbs. white vinegar

3 Tbs. extra-virgin olive oil

1/2 t. celery salt

1 can (6 oz.) chopped clams with juice

1/4 cup finely diced red bell pepper

1/4 cup finely diced green bell pepper

3 medium scallions, trimmed and finely diced

1/4 cup finely diced red onion

Freshly ground white pepper

Bring 2 quarts of salted water to a boil in a large pot. Add the shrimp and cook for about 2 minutes or until they just turn pink. Do not overcook. Remove the shrimp with a slotted spoon to a side dish and let cool.

Bring the water back to a boil, add the scallops and cook for 1 minute or until they just turn opaque. Do not overcook. Drain well, transfer to a side dish and let cool.

In a large bowl, combine the lemon juice, lime juice, vinegar, oil and celery salt. Whisk until well blended. Dry the seafood thoroughly on paper towels and add to the vinaigrette along with the remaining ingredients. Fold gently but thoroughly and season with salt and freshly ground white pepper. Cover the salad and refrigerate for at least 2 hours or until well chilled.

Serve the salad on a bed of field greens, lightly chilled.

SERVES 8

Randy's Tuna Salad

When making this salad or any other tuna salad for that matter, opt for buying a good quality canned albacore tuna and the best jarred mayonnaise possible. It really makes all the difference.

2 Tbs. freshly squeezed lemon juice

1/4 t. Worcestershire sauce

1/2 cup mayonnaise

1/4 cup celery, finely minced

1/4 cup red onion, finely minced

2 cans (8 oz. each) good quality solid white albacore tuna, drained and lightly crumbled with your fingers

Kosher salt

Freshly ground white pepper

In a medium size mixing bowl, combine the lemon juice, Worcestershire sauce and mayonnaise and whisk until well blended.

Add the celery, onion and tuna, season with salt and pepper and fold gently but thoroughly. Cover and refrigerate for 30 minutes before serving.

SERVES 4 TO 5

Try adding 2 cups of cooked "macaroni" to the finished salad for a delicious cold Macaroni and Tuna Salad.

If you like your tuna salad a little spicy, add a few drops of hot sauce.

Platinum Coast Clam Chowder

Though this hearty chowder may be a New England classic, the Bostonians who frequent our restaurant just can't seem to get enough of our Platinum Coast version. As one of our patrons confesses: "Best I've ever had!" — PAT BEGGAN, NAPLES

5 Tbs. unsalted butter

2 cups diced onions

1 1/2 cups diced celery

1/4 cup all-purpose flour, sifted

3 bottles (8 oz. each) clam juice

Optional: 2 Tbs. clam base

1 t. kosher salt

1 t. freshly ground white pepper

1/2 t. dried thyme

1/2 t. Worcestershire sauce

1 t. Tabasco sauce

2 cups, peeled and cubed, all-purpose potatoes

6 cans (6 oz. each) chopped clams with their liquid

2 cups heavy cream

In a large pot, melt the butter over medium heat. Add the onions and celery and cook, stirring often, until soft but not browned, about 10 minutes. Add the flour and cook, stirring constantly, for 1 minute without browning.

Add the clam juice, optional clam base, salt, pepper, thyme, and Worcestershire and Tabasco sauces and stir until well blended. Bring to a boil, reduce the heat and simmer for 10 minutes.

While the soup is simmering, bring salted water to a boil in a small saucepan, add the potatoes and cook until just tender, about 10 minutes. Drain the potatoes well and add to the soup together with the canned clams and their liquid and heavy cream. Simmer the chowder for 12 minutes longer. Taste and correct the seasoning and serve hot accompanied by oyster crackers.

MAKES 6

From left to right:
Shrimp, Crawfish and Okra Gumbo (page 70),
Island Style Seafood Stew (page 71) and
Shrimp, Corn and Lump Crab Chowder (page 72).

Shrimp, Crawfish and Okra Gumbo

1/2 lb. andouille sausage, cut into small dice

1 1/4 cups canola oil

2 cups all-purpose flour

1 cup diced red bell peppers

1 1/2 cups diced celery

1 cup diced onion

2 cups fresh or frozen okra, cut crosswise into 1/2 inch pieces

3 Tbs. finely minced garlic

3 1/2 qts. beef stock or Chicken Stock, (see recipe page 75)

1/2 Tb. dried thyme

2 Tbs. finely minced fresh basil

2 cups crushed tomatoes

1 cup fresh or frozen corn kernels

1/4 cup Crystal Hot Sauce or other hot sauce

2 Tbs. kosher salt

1/2 t. freshly ground white pepper

1 small bay leaf

1 Tb. Randy's Blackening Spice or other blackening seasoning

1 lb. large shrimp, about 21 to 25 per lb., peeled, deveined and cut in half

1 lb. fresh or frozen crawfish tails, cut in half

1 1/2 cups cooked long grain or converted white rice

1 Tb. gumbo file powder

Place the andouille sausage in a small skillet over medium heat and cook, stirring often, until nicely browned, about 2 minutes. Transfer to a double layer of paper towels and set side.

In a Dutch oven or large heavy casserole, heat the oil over medium-low heat, add the flour and whisk until the mixture becomes thick and smooth. Continue cooking, stirring constantly with a wooden spoon, until the roux becomes a deep hazelnut color and has a toasted, nutty aroma.

Raise the heat to medium, add the peppers, celery, onions and okra and stir constantly until the vegetables begin to brown, about 5 minutes. Add the garlic and cook for 1 minute longer.

Pour in the stock, whisking constantly to prevent lumping, until the mixture is smooth. Add the reserved sausage, thyme, basil, tomatoes, corn, hot sauce, salt, pepper, bay leaf and blackening spice. Bring the gumbo to a boil, reduce the heat to low and simmer, partially covered, for 1 hour.

Add the shrimp, crawfish, cooked rice and file powder and simmer for an additional 10 minutes or until the shrimp are opaque and the gumbo has thickened. Taste and correct the seasoning. Remove and discard the bay leaf and serve the gumbo hot, in warm individual bowls accompanied by a crusty loaf of French bread.

SERVES 6

Our Shrimp, Crawfish and Okra Gumbo pairs well with Bridlewood Syrah, Central Coast California. Taste Profile: berry flavors and fig undertones are held up by soft tannins for a long, satisfying mid-palate ending with a clean finish.

Island Style Seafood Stew

The length of the ingredient list may seem daunting but this gutsy variation on the popular Northeast standard is well worth the effort and is one of my favorite chowder recipes. I guarantee that when you serve it to family and friends, they're bound to say: "Hey, wait! Am I in Manhattan"?

4 Tbs. olive oil

3 Tbs. finely minced garlic

½ cup finely minced onions

1 cup finely diced red bell pepper

2 cups clam juice

⅓ cup dry white wine

¼ cup freshly squeezed lemon juice

½ Tb. dried thyme

¼ Tb. coarsely ground black pepper

1 t. kosher salt

16 little neck clams, well scrubbed

8 large shrimp, preferably pink Gulf shrimp, about 15 per pound, peeled and deveined with tails left on

8 large sea scallops

16 mussels, preferably New Zealand, well scrubbed and beards removed

12 oz. fresh black Grouper filets or other firm fleshed white fish, cut into 12 pieces

20 grape tomatoes cut in half

1 small bunch of scallions, trimmed and sliced thinly on the bias

1½ Tbs. finely minced fresh parsley

In a large 8 quart casserole or stock pot, heat the oil over medium heat. Add the garlic, onions and red pepper and cook, stirring often, for about 5 minutes or until the onions soften. Add the clam juice, wine, lemon juice, thyme, pepper and salt and simmer for 3 minutes.

Place the clams in the pot and cook for 4 minutes. Add the shrimp, scallops, mussels and Grouper and cook, covered, for 6 to 8 minutes until all the fish is opaque and the clams and mussels have opened; discard any that do not. Stir in the tomatoes, scallions and parsley and just heat through. Taste and correct the seasoning and ladle the stew into individual bowls. Serve hot with plenty of crusty garlicky bread to soak up all the flavorful juices.

SERVES 4

Shrimp, Corn and Lump Crab Chowder

It's not a classic corn chowder or only a shrimp chowder or even just a basic crab chowder. We have blended all of these flavors into on delicious "stew" combining all of the elements that you'd expect from the best chowder you could possibly imagine. And don't forget to serve it with old fashioned oyster crackers, for what's a chowder without them?

8 oz. smoked bacon, finely diced

¼ cup unsalted butter

1 medium onion, peeled and finely diced

½ cup dry white wine

¼ cup all-purpose flour

1 qt. heavy cream

2 large Yukon gold potatoes, peeled and finely diced

1 can (15 oz.) cream style corn

2 Tbs. Old Bay Seasoning

1 Tb. fresh thyme leaves

2 Tbs. kosher salt

2 Tbs. coarsely ground black pepper

16 medium shrimp, preferably Gulf, peeled, deveined and cut into small pieces

12 oz. good quality lump crabmeat, all shells removed

In a medium size casserole, add the bacon and cook over medium-low heat until crisp. Add the butter and when melted, add the onions and sauté for 8 to 10 minutes or until soft but not browned.

Raise heat to medium, add the wine, and cook for 3-4 minutes or until reduced by half. Whisk in the flour and cook for 1 minute longer, stirring constantly, without browning. Add the heavy cream, potatoes, corn, Old Bay, thyme and salt and pepper. Bring to a boil, reduce the heat and simmer, partially covered, for 30 to 40 minutes or until the potatoes are tender.

Add the shrimp and crabmeat to the casserole and simmer for 10 minutes longer. Serve the soup hot with oyster crackers.

SERVES 8

Naples Seafood Stew

Kudos to our resident baker, Pete, for developing this hearty, flavorful seafood medley. Who would have thought? And no, you don't have to be a baker to achieve great results.

$\frac{1}{3}$ cup olive oil

1 medium onion, peeled and diced

3 large garlic cloves, peeled and finely minced

1 large red bell pepper, cored, seeded and diced

2 large celery stalks, trimmed and diced

$\frac{1}{2}$ cup finely minced fresh parsley

$\frac{1}{2}$ t. dried sage

$\frac{1}{2}$ t. dried rosemary

$\frac{1}{2}$ t. dried thyme

4 qts. clam juice

$\frac{1}{2}$ cup dry white wine

1 t. chili oil

Salt and freshly ground white pepper

16 little neck clams, well scrubbed

16 mussels, well scrubbed and beards removed

1 lb. good quality lump crabmeat, shells removed

16 medium shrimp, about 36 to 40 per pound, peeled and deveined

1 lb. fresh Grouper filet or other firm fleshed white fish, cut into $1\frac{1}{2}$ inch pieces

In a large 8 quart casserole or stock pot, heat the oil over medium heat. Add the onion and garlic and cook for 5 minutes or until soft but not browned. Add the red pepper, celery, parsley, sage, rosemary and thyme and cook for 4 minutes longer, stirring often.

To the casserole, add the clam juice, wine and the chili oil and season with salt and pepper. Bring to a boil, reduce the heat and simmer, covered for 20 minutes.

Add the clams and mussels to the pot and cook, covered, until all the clams and mussels open; discard any that do not. Add the crabmeat, shrimp and Grouper and simmer, covered, for an additional 10 minutes or until all the fish is opaque; do not overcook. Taste and correct the seasoning and serve hot in individual bowls with a crusty loaf of peasant bread.

SERVES 8

Sherry Infused Conch Chowder

This is one of those chowders that is best made the day before so that the ingredients will have a chance to "marry", creating a well balanced palate of flavors. Hold off on adding the sherry until the next day since it will dissipate during refrigeration. Reheat the chowder slowly over a low flame and add the sherry, yes, all of it. Can you ever add too much?

1/2 cup unsalted butter

5 cups minced conch

1 medium onion,
peeled and finely diced

3 medium carrots,
trimmed, peeled and finely diced

1 medium green bell pepper,
cored, seeded and finely diced

1 medium red bell pepper,
cored, seeded and finely diced

3 t. Old Bay Seasoning

1 t. freshly ground white pepper

1/2 t. dried thyme

1 t. dried oregano

4 qts. water

5 oz. clam base

2 oz. lobster base

4 cups chopped canned plum
tomatoes or fresh tomatoes,
peeled and seeded

2 Tbs. Tabasco sauce

2 cups peeled and cubed,
all-purpose potatoes

2 cups canned cream style corn

1 cup dry sherry

Kosher salt

In a large stock pot, melt the butter over medium heat. Add the conch, onion, carrots and green and red peppers and sauté, stirring often, until lightly browned, about 5 to 6 minutes. Add the Old Bay, white pepper, thyme and oregano and cook for 1 minute longer.

Mix the water together with the clam and lobster base in a large mixing bowl and whisk until well blended. Add to the stock pot together with the tomatoes, hot sauce and potatoes and mix well. Bring the mixture to a boil, reduce the heat and simmer, partially covered, for 1 1/4 hours.

Add the corn and sherry and just heat through. Taste and correct the seasoning, adding salt and more white pepper if desired. Serve hot.

SERVES 12

If you cannot find clam and lobster base in your local supermarket, replace the water and the bases with 4 quarts of Fish Stock, see recipe (page 76) or bottled clam juice.

Chicken Stock

Most homemade chicken stocks typically call for whole chickens but I like to use the dark meat of the chicken, such as thighs and drumsticks which makes for a more robust stock. The most important step in a stock is the first – skimming the stock of all of the gray matter that floats to the surface. These are impurities from the bones and meat of the chicken and if not removed, they will make the stock very cloudy and greasy.

$4^1/_2$ lbs. skinless chicken thighs and drumsticks

$2^1/_2$ qts. water

4 large carrots, peeled and diced

2 large onions, peeled and diced

4 large celery stalks with leaves, diced

1 small dried bay leaf

4 whole sprigs fresh thyme

5 whole black peppercorns

1 Tb. kosher salt

In a large pot, combine all of the ingredients. Bring to a boil slowly and carefully skim the surface to remove all gray foam. Reduce the heat and simmer, covered, for 1 hour and 30 minutes, skimming often. When the stock is done, remove it from the heat and cool, uncovered. This stock as with all other stocks must be cooled uncovered to prevent it from souring.

Strain the stock into a large bowl and when completely cool, refrigerate uncovered overnight. You may remove the meat from the bones and reserve for soup or chicken salad.

The next day, thoroughly degrease the stock, removing and discarding the hardened fat from the surface. Transfer to a large pot, bring back to a boil and pour into 1 quart containers. Again cool the stock uncovered and when completely cool, cover and refrigerate or freeze. If the stock is refrigerated, bring it back to a boil every 3 to 4 days to prevent it from souring. The stock can be frozen successfully for 6 to 8 weeks.

MAKES ABOUT 2 QUARTS

Fish Stock

Of all the stocks, the fish stock cooks in the least amount of time since fish bones are quite delicate. Also, this light stock tends to have the least amount of fat. These are bonuses because you can simply prepare the stock in the morning and use it that same evening in your favorite fish, soup or sauce recipe. Just make sure you give it ample time to cool down so that you can easily remove all excess fat from the surface before using.

2 lbs. fish trimmings, preferably heads and bones from firm-fleshed white fish

2 qts. water

2 large carrots, peeled and diced

1 large onion, peeled and diced

2 large celery stalks with leaves, diced

1 small bay leaf

1 large lemon, quartered

5 whole black peppercorns

½ Tb. kosher salt

Rinse the fish trimmings thoroughly under cold water until completely white and free of blood. Remove and discard the gills and place the trimmings in a large pot together with the remaining ingredients.

Bring to a simmer; do not boil. Reduce the heat and continue to simmer, covered for 45 minutes, skimming carefully every 10 minutes. When the stock is done, remove it from the heat and cool, uncovered.

Strain the stock into a large bowl and when completely cool, refrigerate uncovered overnight.

The next day, thoroughly degrease the stock and transfer it to a large pot. Bring back to a simmer and pour the stock into 1 quart containers. Again cool the stock uncovered and when completely cool, cover and refrigerate or freeze. The stock can be refrigerated for up to 1 week, returning it to a boil every 2 to days or it can be frozen for up to 6 weeks.

MAKES ABOUT 2 QUARTS

Do not use fish trimmings from "oily" fish such as salmon, tuna or Mahi Mahi. These are much too oily to make a perfect stock, since the natural oils in the fish tend to become rancid quickly. Use only white fleshed fish such as grouper, flounder or cod.

Shrimp Stock

I happen to love this stock for it's versatility. You can use it in shellfish risottos, soups, chowders and in so many other preparations including sauces. For an easy, spur of the moment fish sauce, take 2 cups of shrimp stock and reduce it over low heat to $1/3$ cup. Whisk in about 6 tablespoons of cold butter, a couple tablespoons of heavy cream and a squeeze of lemon. Season with a little salt and pepper and a few tablespoons of fresh herbs and you're good to go.

$2^1/_2$ Tbs. canola oil

1 medium onion,
peeled and finely diced

2 large carrots,
peeled and finely diced

1 lb. shrimp shells

2 Tbs. tomato paste

2 oz. dried shrimp

1 cup dry sherry

$2^1/_2$ qts. Chicken Stock,
(see recipe page 75)

3 whole sprigs fresh thyme

1 t. kosher salt

1 t. ground white pepper

In a medium pot, heat the oil over high heat. Add the onion, carrots and shrimp shells and sauté until lightly browned, stirring constantly. Add the tomato paste and dried shrimp and sauté for 2 minutes longer, stirring constantly, being careful not to burn the paste.

Add the sherry and cook until reduced to one tablespoon. Add the chicken stock, thyme and salt and pepper. Bring to a boil, reduce the heat and simmer, partially covered, for 45 minutes. Strain the stock into a large bowl and discard the shells. When completely cool, refrigerate, uncovered. The stock can be refrigerated for up to 1 week, returning it to a boil every 2 to days or it can be frozen for up to 6 weeks.

MAKES ABOUT 2 QUARTS

For the shrimp shells, ask your local fish monger or local store to save you the shells from the shrimp that they peel to be sold as cooked shrimp. You can find dried shrimp in your local Chinese or Asian market.

fried fish

The "Fishmarket's" Private Stock Double Coating for Frying Fish

I must admit that my breading for fried fish is probably the best I've ever tasted…if I do say so myself. It has all the elements that you look for in a great coating: it's crisp and crunchy yet light and moist and the secret, in part, is in the double dipping, first in a buttermilk batter and then into a cornmeal/flour mixture.

Also, I base the success of any fried fish on how "greasy" or hopefully not, it is and this relies on two things. One being the freshness of the oil: if the oil has been reused over and over again, it becomes over-saturated with protein from the fish, making the oil much too dense to be used and the batter starts absorbing the old oil resulting in a very greasy end product. So make sure your oil is fresh. The second factor is the correct temperature of frying: if the fish is fried at too low or too high a temperature, it will also produce a "greasy" result and also one that can be either soggy at a low temp or dry, dark and undercooked at too high a temp. I recommend strongly that you use a candy or deep-fry thermometer for an accurate reading. If you happen to own a deep fryer, all the better since it will automatically retain an even temperature for you.

So the next time you order fried fish in a restaurant and it comes out greasy and heavy, you'll know why and I assure you that this will never happen at the "Fishmarket".

Start by making the moist coating: In a shallow bowl, combine the buttermilk, egg, salt and pepper and whisk until well blended. Set aside.

The dry coating: In a large zip lock bag, combine all of the second coating ingredients and shake until thoroughly mixed.

Heat the oil in a large pot to 375 degrees. Dip your seafood first in the moist batter and then place it in the zip-lock bag with the dry coating and shake gently to coat evenly. Place the fish in the hot oil in batches and fry 30 seconds for calamari, 1 to 2 minutes for thin filets, shrimp and scallops and other shellfish and about 3 to 5 minutes for thick filets. Drain well on paper towels, sprinkle with a little additional kosher salt and serve hot with any of our dipping sauces, chutneys or relishes.

BREADING FOR 2 TO 3 LBS. OF SEAFOOD

Soy flour is available in health food stores or in the "health food" section of most supermarkets. You can also substitute more all-purpose flour for the soy flour.

Fried Scallops

The best way in the world to eat a scallop is right from the shell that has been just plucked from the sea… if you're so fortunate. But because scallops do not hold their shells tightly closed, they die super quickly when removed from the water which is why most scallops are sold already shucked.

The bay scallop is the smallest of the scallops, coming from the East Coast, and available seasonally. They are quite small, about $1/2$ inch in diameter and are very sweet and quite tender which makes them a perfect choice for marinating raw for seviche or lightly poached for salads and rice and pasta dishes. The sea scallop, which can be more than twice as large, measuring 1 to $1^3/4$ inches in diameter, comes from either the Atlantic or Pacific oceans and they're usually available all year round. They have a sweet and a velvety smooth texture and are perfect for deep-frying, pan-searing and grilling. Both scallops, in general, should be cream-colored to ivory or pink, not gray or pure white and they should be translucent.

Regardless of which scallop you choose to buy, make sure that they are NOT previously frozen, so ask your fishmonger or supermarket before purchasing. The results, otherwise, can be disastrous because frozen scallops will exude a lot of juice when pan-searing, creating a "soupy" mess or if deep-fried they will produce a very soggy coating instead of a nice crisp one.

In the photo, we prepared the scallops by quickly deep-frying them, until they just lost their translucency and served them with our Sweet Pickle Relish Tartar Sauce (page 143) and wedges of fresh lemon. So simple and so delectable.

Scallops pair well with Toad Hollow "Francine's Selection" Chardonnay, Mendocino, California. Taste Profile: green apples, pears and a tinge of citrus showcase this un-oaked Chardonnay. Visit www.toadhollow.com.

Fried Grouper Sandwich

The bass family includes a large group of diverse fish such as the Grouper because of one common characteristic, and that is their very sharp, pointed dorsal fin. All bass have a similar mild flavor, are very lean and their tender yet firm flesh tends to separate into large flakes when cooked.

Groupers are found in the waters of the Gulf of Mexico and South Atlantic which is why we are so fortunate here in South Florida. They're marketed whole as well as in fillets and steaks and their lean, firm flesh is suitable for roasting, broiling, frying, pan-searing or steaming. The grouper's skin, which is very strongly flavored, should always be removed before cooking.

Here at Randy's, we sell a variety of Groupers Black and Red. Black grouper tends to yield a thicker filet which makes it perfect for grilling, steaming and roasting, while Red yield thinner filets that are excellent for quick methods of cooking such as deep-frying and pan-searing.

Our fried Grouper sandwich is so popular in the "Fishmarket" that we can't seem to keep up! We like to deep-fry the Grouper in our "double dip" breading until super crunchy and tender and then serve it with thick slices of red onion and fresh ripe tomatoes and leaves of Boston lettuce on one of our Golden Brown Sandwich Rolls (page 128). Have plenty of lemon wedges on the side which add a nice citrus tang to the fish and oops, how can I forget? And of course, plenty of creamy tartar sauce.

Fried Calamari

The squid is altogether an odd shellfish because it in fact, has no shell! And it's literally a head with feet! Squid are perfectly white with a purple skin and have a delicious mild flavor with a slightly chewy texture. Cooking the calamari, as the Italians call them, is black and white. There is NO in between. They are cooked either extremely quickly, no more than 30 seconds if sautéing or frying, or they are braised, covered, typically in some sort of tomato sauce, for a long period of time, usually an hour or more to tenderize them. Whether they are fried or sautéed for too long, or they are not braised long enough, they will be tough like rubber, so be careful not to overcook them or undercook them depending upon the method you may choose.

If you aren't able to buy already cleaned squid, cleaning them yourself is really quite simple, once you get into the swing of it. Pull off the head with tentacles and most of the viscera will follow. Cut off and discard the head saving only the tentacles. Then pull out the long quill, the transparent piece of almost plastic-like cartilage from inside the body and discard. Peel off the purple skin and rinse the calamari thoroughly under cold water to remove any excess viscera and skin. Dry thoroughly on paper towels, cut into flat pieces or crosswise into rings and proceed with your favorite recipe.

I happen to love them simply battered and quickly fried like we did for the photo shoot and served with our Marinara Sauce (page 148) and plenty of lemon wedges and paper napkins.

main dishes

Roasted Grouper with a Crispy Red Onion Crust

For onion lovers there's nothing better on our menu than roasted Gulf Grouper encrusted in a delicate blanket of very thin, pan-charred red onions. When preparing this dish for the photo, we paired it with our lemon butter sauce but it is equally delicious instead, drizzled with a little brown butter or the Balsamic Vinaigrette (page 158).

4 fresh red or black Grouper filets
or other firm-fleshed white fish,
about 6 oz. each

6 flat anchovy filets, drained

2 Tbs. finely minced fresh garlic

2 t. freshly squeezed lemon juice

2 Tbs. dry white wine

1/2 t. kosher salt

1 t. freshly ground white pepper

2 large eggs

1/2 cup all-purpose flour

1 small red onion,
peeled and very thinly sliced

1/4 cup extra-virgin olive oil

2 Tbs. tiny capers, drained

1/2 recipe Lemon Beurre Blanc,
(see recipe page 140)

GARNISH:

3 Tbs. fresh chives,
cut into 1/2 inch pieces

Preheat the oven to 350 degrees. Dry the grouper filets thoroughly on paper towels and set aside.

In the workbowl of a food processor combine the anchovies, garlic, lemon juice, wine, salt and pepper and process until smooth. Transfer the mixture to a shallow bowl, add the eggs and whisk until well blended. Place the flour in another shallow bowl and set aside.

Dip the top of each filet (the fleshy side, not the skin side) lightly in the flour, shaking off the excess, then into the egg mixture. You only want to coat the top of each filet. Transfer the filets to a large plate, arrange the onion slices on top of each filet and pat lightly.

Heat the oil in a large non-stick, oven proof skillet over medium to medium-high heat, add the grouper filets, onion side down, without crowding the skillet and cook until the onions begin to brown, about 2 minutes. Carefully turn the filets over with a large spatula and place the skillet in the center of the preheated oven. Roast the filets for an additional 5 to 7 minutes or until the filets are opaque throughout.

Remove the filets from the oven and transfer to warm individual serving plates. Add the capers to the lemon sauce. Spoon some of the sauce around the grouper and garnish with a sprinkling of fresh chives. Serve at once.

SERVES 4

Neapolitan Pan-Seared Grouper

Although this recipe gives you directions for pan-searing the Grouper, we decided to grill it for our photo shoot so that you could see how it lends itself to a variety of cooking methods. For grilling the Grouper, follow the instructions in the Caribbean Grilled Grouper with Fresh Mango Sauce recipe (page 114).

THE VEGETABLES:

3 Tbs. olive oil

1 Tb. finely minced garlic

1 medium onion, peeled and finely diced

8 medium mushrooms, stemmed and sliced

2 cans (8 oz. each) artichoke hearts, drained and halved

1 large ripe tomato, peeled, seeded and diced

1 Tb. finely minced fresh basil

Kosher salt and freshly ground white pepper

THE GROUPER:

4 fresh Grouper filets or other firm-fleshed white fish, about 6 oz. each

Kosher salt and freshly ground white pepper

1/2 cup all-purpose flour

3 Tbs. peanut oil

Start by preparing the vegetables: In a 10 inch skillet, heat the oil over medium-high heat. Add the garlic, onions and mushrooms and cook, stirring often, until the vegetables begin to brown. Reduce the heat, add the artichokes, tomatoes and basil, season with salt and pepper and cook for another 3 to 4 minutes or until the juices have reduced. Keep warm.

The Grouper: Dry the Grouper filets thoroughly on paper towels. Season the filets with salt and pepper and dredge lightly in the flour, shaking off the excess. Heat the oil in a large non-stick skillet over medium heat, add the filets without crowding the skillet and cook for 3 to 4 minutes or until golden brown. Carefully turn the filets over with a large spatula and continue cooking for another 3 to 4 minutes or until the filets are cooked through and golden brown on both sides.

Transfer the filets to individual warm serving plates, spoon some of the vegetables around each portion and serve hot.

SERVES 4

Wild Salmon with Mushrooms, Gorgonzola Dolce and Balsamic Drizzle

My first choice in choosing the kind of salmon for this dish is wild salmon but you can easily substitute a good farm-raised variety. By the way, you don't have to be limited to serving the mushroom "ragout" with only salmon. It works well with other sautéed fish and chicken dishes.

THE DRIZZLE:

6 Tbs. balsamic vinegar

6 Tbs. honey

2 t. coarsely cracked black pepper

THE MUSHROOMS:

2 Tbs. olive oil

5 large garlic cloves, peeled and finely minced

1/2 lb. white mushrooms, wiped, stemmed and sliced

1/2 lb. shiitake mushrooms, stemmed and sliced

3 Portobello mushrooms, stemmed, quartered and sliced

Salt and freshly ground black pepper

2 Tbs. finely minced fresh basil

1/4 cup dry white wine

1/3 cup Chicken Stock, (see recipe page 75)

8 Tbs. (1 stick) unsalted butter

THE SALMON:

12 wild salmon filets (about 2 to 3 oz. each), skinless and preferably center cut

6 Tbs. olive oil

12 oz. Gorgonzola Dolce cheese or other creamy blue cheese, chilled and cut into 12 pieces

Start by preparing the drizzle: In a small bowl combine the balsamic vinegar, honey and cracked pepper and whisk until well blended. Set aside.

The mushrooms: Heat the oil over medium-high heat in a large sauté pan. Add the garlic and mushrooms, season with salt and pepper and cook for 5 minutes, stirring constantly, until the mushrooms begin to brown. Add the basil, wine and stock, bring to a boil and cook until the liquid has reduced to 1 tablespoon. Reserve the mixture in the skillet.

The Salmon: Dry the salmon filets well on paper towels. Heat the oil in a large non-stick skillet over high heat. Add the salmon filets, without crowding the skillet, and sear for 1 to 2 minutes on each side or until medium rare. You might have to sear the salmon in two skillets.

Just before the salmon is done, reheat the mushrooms over medium heat, add the butter and just before the butter has completely melted, remove the skillet from the heat.

When the filets are medium rare, transfer 2 filets to the center of each of 6 warm plates. Spoon the mushroom mixture over each portion, top with one piece of the Gorgonzola and drizzle the plate with a little of the balsamic glaze. Serve at once.

SERVES 6

Northwest King Salmon Cakes

This is an adaptation of the crab cakes so popular here in the Southeast and in the mid-Atlantic states. Although we call for King salmon, which is considered to be the best salmon because of its high fat content, lending to its rich flavor and tender meat, any salmon will do fine. As long as the fish is fresh, once it's minced up and blended with the potatoes and all of the spices, the result will be equally as yummy.

½ lb. fresh King Salmon or other fresh salmon, coarsely chopped

3 large scallions, trimmed and finely minced

2 Tbs. finely minced banana pepper, (see remarks)

2 Tbs. finely diced red bell pepper

1 Tb. Old Bay Seasoning

2 cups Panko (Japanese bread crumbs)

1 t. garlic powder

1 large all-purpose potato, peeled, shredded and dried well with paper towels

1 large egg, lightly beaten

Salt and freshly ground white pepper

5 Tbs. canola oil

In a large bowl combine the salmon, scallions, banana and red bell peppers, Old Bay, Panko, garlic powder, potato and egg and mix gently but thoroughly. Divide the mixture evenly into 12 portions. Shape each portion into round or oval patties and flatten slightly.

Heat the oil in a large non-stick skillet over medium heat. When the oil is hot, add the salmon cakes without crowding the skillet and cook for 2 to 3 minutes per side or until golden brown. This may be done in two batches. Serve hot.

SERVES 6

The banana pepper is also called a banana chili or a sweet banana pepper. You can also use a yellow wax pepper as a substitute but it is a bit hotter than the banana pepper so reduce the amount by 1 tablespoon.

Potato and Panko Crusted Salmon with Garlic Butter

Well, here's another prime example of our photo shoot team being their creative selves which led to "spur of the moment" changes on the set. For example, I usually serve this recipe in the restaurant with Grouper but the salmon that day looked so beautiful that the team decided it would visually be a nice substitution for the picture. It just goes to show that recipes are truly only a guideline and that they leave plenty of room for adaptation, spontaneity and creativity.

1/2 cup all-purpose flour

1 Tb. finely minced fresh flat leaf parsley

2 large eggs

1/4 cup half and half

10 oz. Lay's potato chips or other plain chips

1 1/2 cups Panko (Japanese bread crumbs)

1 t. freshly ground white pepper

1 t. garlic powder

4 fresh salmon filets or a firm-fleshed white fish, about 6 oz. each

1/2 cup canola oil

1 recipe Garlic Butter, (see recipe page 138)

In a shallow bowl, combine the flour and parsley and set aside.

Combine the eggs and half and half in another shallow bowl and whisk until well blended. Reserve.

In the workbowl of a food processor, combine the chips, Panko, pepper and garlic powder and pulse until coarsely chopped. Transfer the mixture to a third shallow bowl and set aside.

Dry the salmon filets thoroughly with paper towels. Dredge the filets first in the flour mixture, shaking off the excess. Then dip the filets in the egg wash and finally into the potato chip mixture, patting the mixture lightly on each side of the filets.

Heat the oil in a large non-stick skillet over medium to medium high heat, add the filets without crowding the skillet and cook for 2 to 3 minutes per side or until nicely browned and the fish is opaque throughout. Transfer the filets to paper towels to drain briefly. Serve the filets on individual warm serving plates, drizzled with a little of the garlic butter.

SERVES 4

Nope, that's not a misprint we do call for potato chips here! They add a nice salty crunchy crust which is no wonder why the Grouper tastes so good.

Our Potato Crusted Salmon pairs well with WhiteHaven Sauvignon Blanc, Marlborough, New Zealand. Taste Profile: vibrant, full-flavored wine with an abundance of currant and gooseberry flavors. Classic grassy and ripe citrus accents, this wine refreshes the palate with a clean, lingering finish.

Grilled Shrimp in a Honey/Coffee BBQ Glaze

There are so many ways to thread shrimp onto skewers for grilling. One example is the method used in my Coconut Crusted Shrimp recipe (page 41). Another way is to take two skewers and place them side by side about ¾ inch apart. Then thread a shrimp onto both skewers simultaneously with head end through one skewer and tail end through the other. Thread these skewers with 3 more shrimp in the same manner to create a "ladder" effect. Continue making these skewered shrimp "ladders" using 2 skewers for each of 4 shrimp. With this method, the skewered shrimp will be easier to handle since they will lay flat for even grilling.

4 doz. shrimp, preferably pink Gulf shrimp, about 15 per pound, peeled, deveined with tails left on

2 Tbs. honey

2 Tbs. strong prepared coffee

½ cup olive oil

2 Tbs. freshly squeezed lemon juice

2 Tbs. Tabasco sauce

2 Tbs. finely minced garlic

2 Tbs. ketchup

1 Tb. red wine vinegar

1 t. dried thyme

1 t. kosher salt

1 t. coarsely cracked black pepper

4 Tbs. Gator Hammock Sauce or other hot sauce

2 Tbs. finely chopped fresh cilantro

12 (12 inch long) wooden skewers

In a large bowl, combine all of the ingredients except for the shrimp and whisk until well blended. Add the shrimp, making sure to coat them well with the marinade, cover and refrigerate over night.

The next day, soak the wooden skewers in water for 1 hour before using.

Prepare the gas or charcoal grill at least 30 minutes before serving.

Remove the shrimp from the marinade and thread 4 shrimp on each skewer. Place the shrimp kebabs on the gas grill or directly over the hot coals of a charcoal grill and cook 2 to 3 minutes per side or until the shrimp just turn opaque. Be careful not to burn. Remove from the grill and serve hot.

SERVES 6

Black Peppercorn and Sesame Crusted Ahi Tuna (page 60)
served on a bed of our Island Rice Pilaf (page 163) and
accompanied by wasabi and soy sauce.

Garlicky Steamed Mussels

When looking at the photo, you can see that we prepared the mussels "on the half shell" which is a little time consuming but makes for a more elegant and unique dish. Before adding the butter and parsley to the pot in the third step, remove the mussels from the pot and remove and discard the empty half shell from each mussel. Return them to the pot, and proceed with the recipe. The presentation will definitely "wow" your guests.

5 lbs. fresh mussels,
well scrubbed and beards removed

1 Tb. all-purpose flour

4 Tbs. olive oil

10 large garlic cloves,
peeled and finely chopped

2 t. coarsely cracked black pepper

1/4 cup dry white wine

4 Tbs. unsalted butter

2 Tbs. finely minced fresh parsley

Place the mussels in a large bowl. Cover them with water, add the flour to the water and let the mussels soak for 15 minutes. Drain the mussels, rinse well and set aside.

In a large casserole, heat the oil over medium heat. Add the garlic and cook, stirring often, for 1 minute. Add the cracked pepper, white wine and mussels to the casserole, cover tightly and steam for 8 to 10 minutes, occasionally shaking the pan back and forth, until the mussels open; discard any mussels that do not open.

Uncover the pan, add the butter and parsley to the pan juices and toss well with the mussels. Serve immediately with crispy garlic bread for mopping up the sauce. Don't forget to pass plenty of napkins!

SERVES 4

By soaking the mussels in water with a bit of flour helps the mussels disgorge any of the sand that may be trapped in their shells. Also the mussels will absorb the flour and become a little larger and plumper which will keep them nice and moist when steamed.

Gratin of Florida Seafood

What I like best about this kind of dish is that you can prepare it in advance up to the point of baking. Transfer the mixture to the gratin dish, cover and refrigerate until needed. Then uncover the dish and proceed with the recipe, allowing for an additional 5 minutes of baking time to compensate for the chilling of the gratin. Also, feel free to substitute any other fresh herbs for the thyme, such as dill, parsley or chives or a mixture of all three. Experiment with the sauce. It's quite good-natured.

4 Tbs. unsalted butter

2 Tbs. all-purpose flour

2 Tbs. dry sherry

2 1/2 cups half and half

1 Tb. finely minced garlic

1 t. fresh or dried thyme

Kosher salt and freshly ground white pepper

1 1/2 cups Monterey Jack cheese, grated

1 lb. fresh Grouper filets or other firm-fleshed white fish, cut into 1 1/2 inch pieces

8 large shrimp, preferably pink Gulf shrimp, about 16 to 20 per pound, peeled, deveined and cut in half

8 large sea scallops, quartered

1 t. sweet paprika

In a 2 quart saucepan, melt 2 tablespoons of the butter over medium heat. Add the flour and cook for 1 minute, stirring constantly, without browning. Whisk in the sherry and half and half. Bring to a boil, reduce the heat and simmer for 5 minutes, whisking often. Stir in the garlic, thyme and 1 cup of the cheese. Season with salt and pepper and simmer, stirring constantly, until the cheese has just melted. Remove the pan from the heat and set the sauce aside.

Preheat the oven to 400 degrees.

Dry the Grouper, shrimp and scallops thoroughly on paper towels. Melt the remaining butter in a large non-stick skillet over medium heat. Add all of the seafood and cook, stirring gently, until the fish just turns opaque, about 3 to 4 minutes. Remove the skillet from the heat, add the reserved sauce and fold gently but thoroughly.

Divide the seafood mixture equally among 4 individual gratin dishes or one large gratin dish or casserole. Sprinkle with the remaining cheese, dust with the paprika and place the dishes in the center of the preheated oven. Bake for about 12 to 15 minutes or until golden brown and bubbly. Serve hot.

SERVES 4

Platinum Coast Grouper Stir-fry

Stir Fry dishes are all about the prep work. It takes so much longer to prep than to actually cook them, so make sure you have all of your ingredients ready to go and the rest is easy.

¼ cup all-purpose flour

¼ cup cornstarch

1½ lbs. fresh Grouper filets or other firm-fleshed white fish, cut into 2 inch pieces

8 Tbs. canola oil

1 Tb. finely minced fresh ginger

1 Tb. finely minced garlic

¼ lb. sugar snap peas, strings removed

¼ lb. thin asparagus, peeled and cut into 2 inch lengths

1 cup mung bean sprouts

1 small bunch of scallions, trimmed and sliced thinly on the bias

1 t. sesame oil

1 t. chili oil

2 Tbs. oyster sauce

1 Tb. soy sauce

Optional: 1 Tb. dry sherry

1 cup Randy's Brown Sauce, (see recipe page 145)

2 t. sesame seeds, lightly toasted

In a medium size mixing bowl, combine the flour and cornstarch and whisk until well blended. Set aside.

Heat 6 tablespoons of the oil in a large skillet or wok over high heat. Dredge the Grouper in the flour mixture, shaking off the excess and add to the hot oil. Fry the fish until golden brown on all sides. You might have to fry the fish in batches. Remove the fish with a slotted spoon to paper towels and reserve.

Discard the oil from the skillet and wipe clean. Reduce the heat to medium-high and add the remaining oil to the skillet. When the oil is hot, add the ginger, garlic, snap peas and asparagus and toss constantly for 2 minutes. Add the bean sprouts, scallions, sesame oil, chili oil, oyster sauce, soy sauce and optional sherry and toss well into the vegetables. Fold in the brown sauce together with the Grouper, being careful not to break apart the fish and cook for another 3 to 4 minutes, tossing the mixture often. Transfer the stir-fry to a serving platter, sprinkle with the sesame seeds and serve hot accompanied by steamed rice.

SERVES 4

Fettuccine with Garlic Shrimp Alfredo

The success of the classic Alfredo sauce is determined by the quality of the cheese. Use only top quality Parmesan, preferably Parmigiano-Reggiano, which is the only true Parmesan sold in this country. You can tell its authenticity by the fact that its name is stenciled into the yellow rind of the cheese. Purchase the cheese in one piece and grate it as you need it. It will be that much more moist, creating a creamier, tastier sauce.

$1\frac{1}{2}$ lbs. dried fettuccine

Kosher salt

3 Tbs. olive oil

2 lbs. large shrimp, about 21 to 25 per pound, peeled and deveined

16 Tbs. (2 sticks) unsalted butter

3 large garlic cloves, peeled and finely minced

4 cups heavy cream

8 oz. freshly grated Pecorino Romano cheese

Freshly ground white pepper

GARNISH:

3 Tbs. finely minced fresh parsley

$\frac{3}{4}$ cup freshly grated Parmesan cheese

Bring plenty of salted water to a boil in a large pot; add the fettuccine and cook for 6 to 8 minutes or until barely tender, "al dente". Drain well but do not rinse. Toss with 1 tablespoon of the oil and set aside.

Dry the shrimp thoroughly on paper towels. Heat the remaining oil in a 12 inch skillet over medium heat. Add the shrimp and sauté for 1 to 2 minutes or until they just turn pink. Do not overcook. Transfer the shrimp with a slotted spoon to a side dish and reserve.

Add the butter to the skillet and when it has just melted, stir in the garlic and cook for 1 minute without browning. Add the heavy cream, bring to a simmer and reduce by $\frac{1}{4}$ or until the sauce starts to thicken, whisking often. Whisk in the Romano cheese, season with salt and pepper and cook until the cheese has melted.

Return the shrimp to the skillet together with the cooked pasta and toss well with the sauce. Simmer for 1 to 2 minutes longer or until just heated through. Serve at once on warm individual plates, sprinkled with the parsley and generous portion of Parmesan cheese.

SERVES 6

Ross' Old Bay Soft Shell Crabs in a Pecan Sauce

Soft-shell crabs are blue crabs in the stage between shedding its shell and growing back a new one, a process the crab repeats a dozen times throughout its life. These crabs are only in this interim stage for one week, which makes them tricky to harvest and available only seasonally. So when you see fresh soft-shell crabs at the market, snatch them up and try out this recipe. Our Chef Ross came up with a unique nutty, creamy sauce to accompany them, one that is sure to become a favorite.

¼ cup all-purpose flour

1 t. Old Bay Seasoning

1 t. coarsely ground black pepper

4 soft shell crabs, cleaned

4 Tbs. canola oil

2 Tbs. unsalted butter

1 oz. chopped pecans

1 t. freshly squeezed lemon juice

½ cup heavy cream

Kosher salt and freshly ground black pepper

1 Tb. finely minced fresh parsley

In a shallow bowl, combine the flour, Old Bay and black pepper and mix well. Set aside.

Heat the oil in a large skillet over medium-high heat. Dredge the crabs in the flour mixture, shaking off the excess and add to the hot oil without crowding the skillet. Cook for 3 to 4 minutes per side or until golden brown.

Remove the crabs from the skillet and transfer to individual serving plates and keep warm. Pour out and discard the excess fat from the skillet and wipe the skillet clean. Reduce heat to medium, add the butter and pecans to the skillet and sauté for 1 minute, being careful not to burn. Add the lemon juice and heavy cream, season with salt and pepper and cook for 5 minutes, whisking constantly, until slightly reduced. Add the parsley to the pecan cream and spoon some of the sauce over the crabs. Serve at once.

SERVES 2 AS A MAIN COURSE OR 4 AS AN APPETIZER

Sautéed Pink Gulf Shrimp Scampi

It was 4 a.m., yes that's right 4 a.m., on the fourth day of photography for the cookbook. We were working so early because we could only shoot after we closed the restaurant for the day since we were shooting right in the restaurant! We had been going strong for almost 8 hours and now everyone was tired and hungry but plugging away to beat the deadline. When out comes Hector, one of our chefs that helped prepare the food pictured here, to save the day with plenty of hot food to boost our energy level and one of the dishes he presented was this delectable shrimp scampi. Our stylist said that it looked so beautiful that we had to photograph it and so we did, right there on the spot! Thanks Hector for reviving us and for contributing to one of the great pictures in the book.

20 large shrimp, preferably pink Gulf shrimp, about 15 per pound, peeled and deveined with tails left on

$1/3$ cup all-purpose flour

$2^{1}/_{2}$ Tbs. unsalted butter

3 Tbs. finely minced garlic

1 t. kosher salt

2 t. coarsely cracked black pepper

$1^{1}/_{4}$ cups dry white wine

$1/4$ cup freshly squeezed lemon juice

1 Tb. finely minced fresh parsley

Dry the shrimp thoroughly on paper towels. Dredge lightly in the flour, shaking off the excess.

Melt the butter over medium-high heat in a large skillet and when hot, add the shrimp together with the garlic, salt and pepper and sauté for 3 minutes, stirring often. Add the wine and lemon juice, reduce the heat and simmer until the shrimp are fully cooked and opaque and sauce has thickened, about 2 to 3 minutes longer. Sprinkle with the parsley and serve hot accompanied by toasted peasant bread or crostini to soak up all of the wonderful sauce.

SERVES 4

shmarket Restau...
na "Old Florida charm! Have...
ous seafood, and our own special Key Lime Pie, th...
Randy's features the freshest seafood, caught dai...
wn in fresh from the icy waters of New...
...verages will compliment your m...
...So kick back and re...
...Randy's Fishm...

Filet of Grouper with Pistachio Crumble

The unique pairing of fresh Florida Grouper and crispy pistachios has made this one of the most requested dishes in our restaurant. The recipe happens to be quite simple and can easily be duplicated at home but don't limit yourself to just coating Grouper! The crumble works perfectly fine on other firm fleshed fish as well.

4 fresh red or black Grouper filets or other firm-fleshed white fish, about 6 oz. each

2 slices (4 oz.) of 8 Grain Sourdough Bread (see recipe page 132) or other hearty multi-grain bread

1/2 cup shelled unsalted pistachios, about 5 oz.

1 t. kosher salt

1/2 t. freshly ground white pepper

1/2 cup all-purpose flour

1/2 cup half and half

1/4 cup canola oil

1/2 recipe Lemon Beurre Blanc, (see recipe page 140)

GARNISH:

Fresh sprigs of cilantro

Preheat the oven to 350 degrees. Dry the grouper filets thoroughly on paper towels and set aside.

Lightly toast the bread until dry and add it to the workbowl of a food processor together with the pistachios, salt and pepper. Pulse until coarsely chopped. Transfer the mixture to a shallow bowl. Place the flour in another shallow bowl and the half and half in a third bowl.

Dip the top of each filet (the fleshy side, not the skin side) lightly in the flour, shaking off the excess, then into the half and half and finally coat the top of each filet with the pistachio mixture. You only want to coat the top of the filets.

Heat the oil in a large non-stick, oven proof skillet over medium to medium heat, add the grouper filets, pistachio side down, without crowding the skillet and cook, until lightly browned, about 2 minutes. Carefully turn the filets over with a large spatula and place the skillet in the center of the preheated oven. Roast the filets for an additional 5 to 7 minutes or until the filets are opaque throughout.

Remove the filets from the oven and transfer to warm individual serving plates. Spoon some of the beurre blanc on each plate and garnish with a fresh sprigs of cilantro. Serve at once.

SERVES 4

Caribbean Grilled Grouper with Fresh Mango Sauce

4 Tbs. each, very finely diced fresh mango, fresh papaya and fresh cantaloupe

4 fresh Grouper filets or other firm-fleshed white fish filets, about 8 oz. each

Kosher salt

Freshly ground white pepper

4 Tbs. peanut oil

1 cup Fresh Mango Beurre Blanc, (see recipe page 140)

GARNISH:

Sprigs of fresh cilantro

In a small bowl combine the mango, papaya and melon, mix well and reserve.

Prepare the gas or charcoal grill and preheat the oven to 400 degrees.

Pat the Grouper filets dry with paper towels. Brush each side with a little peanut oil and season with salt and white pepper. Brush the grill with some oil and place the filets on the hot gas grill or directly above the hot coals of a charcoal grill and cook for 1 minute per side or until the fish has nice brown grill marks; when turning the delicate fillets use a large metal spatula which will make the procedure easier.

Remove the filets from the grill and place them on a heavy baking sheet. Set the baking sheet in the center of the preheated oven and roast for 6 to 8 minutes or until the filets are cooked through. You can test for doneness by inserting the tip of a sharp knife in the thickest portion of the filets. If the filets are an opaque white, they are done. Do not overcook.

Transfer the filets to individual warm serving plates and spoon 1/4 cup of the mango sauce around each. Sprinkle the sauce with a little of the diced fruit mixture, garnish with sprigs of cilantro and serve hot.

SERVES 4

The filets can also be pan-seared. Dredge the fish lightly in some all-purpose flour, shaking off the excess. Heat 3 tablespoons of peanut oil in a large non-stick skillet over medium heat. Add the filets, without crowding the skillet and cook for 3 to 4 minutes. Carefully turn the filets over with a large spatula and continue cooking for another 3 to 4 minutes or until the filets are cooked through and golden brown on both sides. Test for doneness following directions above. Continue with the above recipe and serve as directed.

Butterflied and Baked Colossal Shrimp with a Crabmeat Filling

I may seem biased, but I firmly believe that our stuffing for shrimp is the best ever. So many restaurants use those dreadful poultry-seasoned, turkey stuffing croutons for their filling which I thoroughly detest. At Randy's, we use crispy Ritz crackers, lots of butter and garlic and tons of good lump crabmeat making the end result irresistible.

1 lb. good quality lump crabmeat, shells removed

6 Tbs. unsalted butter, melted

3 Tbs. finely minced scallions

1 t. Old Bay Seasoning

1 t. Worcestershire sauce

1 Tb. Crystal hot sauce or other hot sauce

2 Tbs. mayonnaise

1/2 t. garlic powder

1 1/2 cups Ritz crackers, crushed

1/4 cup dry sherry

2 t. kosher salt

1 t. freshly ground white pepper

32 colossal shrimp, preferably pink Gulf shrimp, about 15 per pound, peeled, with tails on

ACCOMPANIMENT:

Lemon wedges

Melted salted butter

In a large bowl, combine all of the ingredients except for the shrimp and mix well. Cover and refrigerate until needed.

Preheat the oven to 350 degrees

Butterfly the shrimp: lay the shrimp on its side on a cutting board. Starting about 1/4 inch from the tail, make a horizontal cut with a sharp knife along the outside curve of each shrimp, being careful not to cut all the way through the shrimp but just enough so that they can be opened for stuffing. With your fingers, open each shrimp and flatten slightly.

Transfer the butterflied shrimp to a lightly greased shallow baking dish in a single layer, cut side up, so that they lie flat. Season with salt and pepper and divide the stuffing evenly among the shrimp, pressing lightly.

Place the baking dish in the center of the preheated oven and bake the shrimp for 15 minutes or until the stuffing is golden brown and the shrimp are opaque. Remove from the oven, transfer to warm individual serving plates and serve hot with wedges of lemon and melted butter.

SERVES 8

Georgi's Cheesy Shrimp and Lump Crabmeat Enchiladas

The slow cooked onions, roasted red peppers and the delicate shrimp and crabmeat all lend themselves to an incredible melding of flavors. This dish is a hit every time I serve it and has become a dinner party favorite.

THE TORTILLAS:

8 Tbs. corn oil

12 (8-inch) flour tortillas

THE FILLING:

2 Tbs. unsalted butter

1 large Vidalia or other sweet onion, peeled and finely diced

1 cup diced raw shrimp, preferably Gulf shrimp

1 cup good quality lump crabmeat, shells removed

1/2 cup diced roasted red peppers or pimientos

8 oz. cream cheese, softened

Salt and freshly ground black pepper

1 1/2 cups heavy cream

2 cups shredded Monterey Jack cheese

GARNISH:

1/4 cup fresh cilantro leaves

1/2 cup diced black olives

2 limes cut into 12 wedges

Preheat the oven to 375 degrees.

Start by preparing the tortillas: In a 10 inch non-stick skillet heat 2 teaspoons of the oil over medium-high heat. When the oil is hot, add one tortilla and fry quickly on both sides for a just few seconds. Do not fry the tortilla until crisp; you want it to just soften. Transfer the tortilla to lightly damp paper towels. Wrap in the towels to keep it soft and pliable and continue frying the remaining tortillas in the same manner using 2 teaspoons of oil for each. Keep them stacked and wrapped in the paper towels until needed.

The filling: Wipe the skillet clean with paper towels. Add the butter and melt over medium-low heat. Add the onion and cook until soft but not browned, about 5 minutes, stirring often. Add the shrimp and continue to cook, stirring often, until the shrimp turn bright pink and are no longer translucent, about 2 to 3 minutes longer.

Remove the skillet from the heat and add the crabmeat and red peppers and toss lightly. Transfer the mixture to a large mixing bowl, add the softened cream cheese and fold gently so as not to break up the crabmeat. Season the mixture with salt and pepper.

Unwrap the tortillas and place about 1/3 cup of the seafood filling down the center of each tortilla. Roll up like a cigar to enclose the filling and place the tortillas seam side down and side by side, snugly in a rectangular baking dish in one layer. You can cover the enchiladas and refrigerate them at this point if making ahead.

Pour the heavy cream over the enchiladas and sprinkle with the cheese. Place the dish in the center of the preheated oven and bake uncovered, for 20 minutes or until golden brown and bubbly. If the enchiladas were chilled, you will need to bake them for 30 minutes instead and covered for the first 15 minutes.

Remove from the oven and garnish with cilantro and olives. Don't forget to pass the lime wedges to squeeze over each portion. The fresh lime juice brings all the incredible flavors of this dish together. Serve at once with a well-seasoned green salad.

SERVES 6

You can substitute bay scallops for the shrimp or use a firm fleshed fish such as Grouper cut into bite size pieces. And for a variation, replace all of the shellfish with 2 large boneless chicken breasts, poached or steamed and torn into shreds.

Spicy South Florida Lump Crab Cakes

My South Florida crab cakes are so convincingly delicious that I bet blindfolded, you couldn't tell the difference between mine and Maryland crab cakes! Try them out and judge for yourself.

1/2 cup unsalted butter

1/4 cup finely minced celery

1/4 cup finely minced onion

1/4 cup Old Bay Seasoning

1 1/2 Tbs. onion powder

1 1/2 Tbs. dry mustard

1 Tb. granulated garlic

2 Tbs. freshly squeezed lemon juice

2 t. Worcestershire sauce

1/2 cup mayonnaise

*1/2 to 3/4 cup Panko
(Japanese bread crumbs)*

*2 lbs. good quality lump crabmeat,
all shells removed*

*Kosher salt and freshly ground
black pepper*

*1 recipe Randy's Mustard/Lemon
Sauce for Crab Cakes,
(see recipe page 144)*

In a small skillet melt 1/4 cup of the butter over low heat. Add the onion and celery and cook until soft but not browned. Transfer the mixture to a large bowl and set aside to cool completely.

Add the Old Bay, onion powder, mustard, garlic, lemon juice, Worcestershire, mayonnaise and 1/2 cup of the Panko to the bowl with the onion mixture and mix well. Fold in the crabmeat gently but thoroughly. Do not over mix or the crabmeat will lose it's shape. If the mixture is too loose, add the remaining Panko.

Divide the crab mixture into 16 portions and with your hands, form into thick round or oval shapes. Place the cakes on a parchment lined cookie sheet and set aside.

Melt the remaining butter in a large non-stick skillet over medium heat. When the butter is hot, add the crab cakes without crowding the skillet and cook until golden brown on both sides. You may need to do this step in two batches. Remove from the skillet and sprinkle with a little kosher salt and black pepper. Serve at once with the mustard/lemon sauce.

SERVES 8

You can freeze the crab cakes, uncooked, successfully. Place the crab cakes on a parchment lined cookie sheet and set in the freezer. When completely frozen, transfer the crab cakes to zip-lock bags and return to the freezer. When ready to serve, remove the cakes from the freezer and let thaw completely. Proceed with step 4 of the preparation.

Our Spicy South Florida Lump Crab Cakes pair well with Duck Pond Pinot Gris, Williamette Valley, Oregon. Taste Profile: nose of peach, vanilla and limes opulent mouth feel and gorgeous fresh-fruit palate.

Black and "Blue" Grouper

4 fresh Grouper filets or
other firm-fleshed white fish
filets, about 8 oz. each

2 Tbs. Randy's Blackening Spice
or other blackening spice mix

2 Tbs. peanut oil

8 Tbs. Randy's Blue Cheese Dressing,
(see recipe page 159)

4 Tbs. crumbled blue cheese

Pat the Grouper filets dry with paper towels and sprinkle each side with some of the blackening spice.

Heat the oil in a non-stick skillet over medium heat. Add the filets, without crowding the skillet and cook for 3 to 4 minutes. Carefully turn the filets over with a large spatula and continue cooking for another 3 to 4 minutes or until the filets are cooked through. You can test for doneness by inserting the tip of a sharp knife in the thickest portion of the filets. If the filets are an opaque white, they are done. Do not overcook.

Transfer the filets to individual serving plates. Spoon 2 tablespoons of blue cheese dressing over each filet, sprinkle with 1 tablespoon of the crumbled blue and serve at once.

SERVES 4

Our "House Special" Seafood Penne

1 each, medium yellow and red bell pepper, cored, seeded and cut into matchsticks

1 cup broccoli florets

1 large carrot, trimmed, peeled and cut into matchsticks

1½ cups sugar snap peas, strings removed

2 small yellow squash, trimmed and cut into matchsticks

Salt

1 lb. penne

¾ cup Garlic, Onion and Ginger Oil, (see recipe page 139)

24 large shrimp, about 21 to 25 per pound, peeled and deveined

8 oz. fresh Grouper or other firm fleshed fish, cut into 1½ inch pieces

12 large sea scallops

8 oz. calamari, cleaned, cut into rings including tentacles

1 medium onion, peeled and finely diced

1¾ cups Randy's Brown Sauce, (see recipe page 145)

2½ Tbs. oyster sauce

2½ t. soy sauce

1 t. sesame oil

3 Tbs. dry white wine

Freshly ground black pepper

1 cup finely grated Parmesan cheese

Fill a large mixing bowl with ice water and set aside. Bring plenty of salted water to a boil in a large pot, add the bell peppers, broccoli and carrots and cook for 30 seconds. Add the snap peas and squash and cook for 1 minute longer or until the vegetables are crisp tender. Immediately drain the vegetables and plunge them into the ice water to stop further cooking. When cool, drain and dry well with paper towels. Reserve.

Again bring salted water to a boil in a large pot; add the penne and cook for 6 to 8 minutes or until barely tender, "al dente". Drain well but do not rinse. Toss with 1 tablespoon of the garlic oil and set aside.

Heat the remaining garlic oil in a large skillet (12 to 14 inches) over medium heat. When just hot, add the shrimp, Grouper, scallops and calamari and cook, stirring constantly, for about 2 minutes. Add the onions and blanched vegetables and cook quickly, for another 2 minutes, tossing with the seafood. Reduce the heat and add the brown sauce, oyster sauce, soy sauce, sesame oil, wine and pasta. Season with salt and pepper and simmer, tossing well with the sauce, for 2 to 3 minutes longer or until just heated through. Do not overcook.

Transfer the pasta to a large serving bowl, sprinkle generously with the Parmesan and serve at once with a warm crusty Italian bread.

SERVES 4 TO 6

Our House Special Seafood Penne pairs well with Maso Canali Pinot Grigio, Trentino, Italy. Taste Profile: the nose delivers peach and a surprising hint of honey, and the wine is characterized by enticing tropical flavors of apricot, lemon and pineapple with floral notes.

breads

Golden Brown Sandwich Rolls

A great sandwich begins with great bread and no matter how terrific the filling, a sandwich cannot reach its highest potential on an inferior slice of bread. That's why we asked Todd Johnson (page 135), to develop a superb roll – crispy on the outside yet moist on the inside, for our very popular and extremely delicious fried Grouper sandwich. So Todd came up with this unique square of golden brown dough which I think is a winner, hands down! Dip fresh Grouper in our Private Stock Coating (page 80) and serve it with slices of ripe tomato, thickly sliced red onions and leaves of Boston lettuce on one of these square treats. Just add a little tartar sauce and a squeeze of fresh lemon and enjoy all of the praise!

$1/4$ oz. active dry yeast

$1 1/2$ oz. olive oil

$1/4$ oz. salt

$1/4$ oz. granulated sugar

12 oz. warm water

$1 1/4$ lbs. bread flour

All-purpose flour for dusting

To the bowl of an electric mixer fitted with a dough hook, combine the yeast, oil, salt, sugar and water and let sit for 10 minutes or until the yeast begins to proof: the mixture will start to bubble.

Add the bread flour and mix on medium speed until smooth and elastic to form a fairly soft dough. Transfer the dough to a lightly floured cookie sheet and press lightly to the thickness of 1 inch. Dust lightly with flour and chill the dough for 30 minutes or until a bit firmer.

Preheat the oven to 400 degrees.

Remove the dough from the cookie sheet and transfer to a lightly floured surface, being careful not to overwork the dough. With a lightly floured rolling pin, roll the dough to a rectangle measuring 12" x 16" and just under $1/2$" thick. With a sharp knife, cut the rectangle into 12, 4 inch squares and sprinkle the tops lightly with flour.

Line the bottom of a large cookie sheet with parchment paper. Carefully transfer the dough squares to the paper about 1 to 2 inches apart. Prick the surface lightly all over with a fork. Place the sheet in the center of the preheated oven and bake for about 12 to 15 minutes or until golden brown. Remove from the oven and let cool. Serve as desired.

MAKES 1 DOZEN

Georgi's Famous Banana Quick Bread

What do you do with really overripe bananas? Never toss them away when you can turn them into our family favorite. This recipe is by far one of the moistest and flavorful banana breads we've ever tried. It's a mainstay at Randy's.

1 Tb. unsalted butter

1½ cups sifted all-purpose flour

1 t. baking soda

¼ t. salt

3 to 4 very ripe bananas, peeled

1 cup granulated sugar

1 whole large egg, lightly beaten

¼ cup canola

Optional: 1 cup chopped walnuts

Preheat the oven to 375 degrees. Using the butter, lightly coat the inside of a standard, 1 pound loaf pan (8¼" x 4¼" x 2½") and set aside.

In a medium-size mixing bowl combine the flour, baking soda and salt, whisk until well blended and reserve.

In a small bowl, mash the banana pulp with the back of a fork and reserve.

Combine the egg and sugar in a large mixing bowl and stir together until smooth. Slowly add the oil, whisking until well blended. Fold in the bananas and optional walnuts. Add the dry ingredients and fold gently but thoroughly until the flour just disappears. Do not over mix.

Fill the prepared loaf pan with the batter and bake in the center of the preheated oven for about 1 hour or until a toothpick when inserted comes out clean. Remove the bread from the oven and let cool completely on a wire cake rack.

Run the edge of a sharp knife around the inside of the pan to loosen the bread. Cut into ½ inch slices and serve with whipped unsalted butter or cream cheese.

MAKES 1 (1 POUND) LOAF

8 Grain Sourdough Bread

This bread is so hearty and healthy that it's difficult to believe something so delicious can be so good for you too!

THE SOUR:

1/4 oz. active dry yeast

6 oz. bread flour

1/2 cup cold water

THE DOUGH:

1 lb. bread flour

1 oz. whole wheat flour

1 oz. wheat bran

1 oz. coarse rye meal

2 cups cold water

1/2 cup honey

1 Tb. salt

2 oz. flax seed

2 oz. millet

2 oz. unsalted sunflower seeds

1 oz. sesame seeds preferably unhulled

4 oz. rolled oats

All-purpose flour for dusting

TOPPING:

Water

Rolled oats

Start by making the sour: The night before preparing the breads, combine the yeast, flour and water in a large mixing bowl and mix into a smooth paste. Let stand overnight at room temperature. Use a large enough mixing bowl to compensate for expansion of the sour.

The next day prepare the dough: Combine all the dough ingredients in the bowl of an electric mixer fitted with the dough hook, add the sour and mix on medium speed for 10 minutes or until well blended. You can also do this in a bread machine following manufacturer's directions.

Transfer the dough to a very large mixing bowl dusted with flour, cover with a clean kitchen towel and let rise in a warm (75-80 degrees) place for 2 hours or until double in size. The top of your refrigerator is a great place or if you have a gas oven, place the bowl in the turned off oven to rise with only the pilot light.

Punch the dough down and transfer to a lightly floured work surface. Divide the dough into 4 equal parts. Shape into ovals or rounds or any other desired shape and place on greased cookie sheets. Lightly brush the tops of each with a little water and sprinkle with some oats. Let rise in a warm spot to 1 1/2 times their original size.

Meanwhile preheat the oven to 400 degrees.

Score the tops of the loaves, crosswise and 1/4 inch deep with a sharp knife and place the loaves in the center of preheated oven. Bake for 25 to 35 minutes or until nicely browned and sounding hollow when tapped on the bottom. If you have a meat thermometer, the internal temperature should be about 195 degrees. Remove from the oven and serve warm or at room temperature with a bowl of good quality unsalted butter.

MAKES 4 LOAVES

Todd Johnson

Since I really don't know much about bread making and just don't have the time or patience for it, I have all of my breads served at my "Fishmarket" restaurant, including our delicious Golden Brown Sandwich Rolls (page 128), the super moist 8-Grain Sourdough Bread (page 132) and all of our luncheon and dinner breads made by pastry chef and bread baker extraordinaire, Todd Johnson. A pastry prodigy by the age of 21, Todd Johnson was born in 1959, the son of parents who appreciated good food and wine. He was raised in an environment where he was encouraged to participate in cooking at an early age.

Upon graduating high school at the tender age of 16, Todd chose to pursue a career in Culinary Arts and headed off to New York to The Culinary Institute of America. He graduated in 1978 after an externship at the famed La Maisonette in Cincinnati, Ohio.

It was at Grand Hotel on Mackinac Island in Michigan that Todd found his true calling in the Pastry Shop. The Executive Pastry Chef there was a 72 year old German named Herman Neibaum who was ready to retire and looking for someone to train as his replacement. Todd spent 2 seasons under his tutelage in both Michigan and Florida before Herman retired and left Todd to manage the staff of 16 in Grand Hotel's pastry shop at the age of 21.

The first season Todd spent in Florida he met his wife Donna, was married within a year and started a family. Sensing that seasonal hotel work in Michigan and Florida was not going to work once the kids were in school, Todd started looking for a place to settle.

It was at this point that he met the second mentor in his life, Norman Love. It was at a small establishment in Fort Myers, Florida named Chateau Robert where Todd was introduced to more contemporary styles of pastry by Norman.

Years later when Norman had gone on to become the Corporate Pastry Chef for The Ritz-Carlton Hotel Company the two were joined again when Todd was hired as the Pastry Chef of the Ritz-Carlton in Naples, Florida.

The two shared an office in the pastry shop in Naples where Norman was based for the next 7 years. While Norman trotted the globe opening hotels and learning tricks of the trade from some of the finest Pastry Chefs in the world, Todd stayed put and ran the operation. The best part of that relationship was that when he returned to Naples, Norman was always eager to teach Todd whatever new techniques he had picked up.

From 2001 through 2005 Todd oversaw a staff of 54 at Atlantis Resort & Casino on beautiful Paradise Island Bahamas. They produce nearly all of the breads, breakfast pastries and desserts for the resort which boasts 34 food and beverage outlets and annual food revenues of 80 to 85 million dollars per year.

Late in 2005 Todd moved back to Florida and opened Artisan Bread Company. His mission is to bring great breads to the consumers of Southwest Florida. Having accumulated 25 years of experience, he brings a wealth of knowledge to this new challenge and so far the results have been outstanding. Featured are natural sourdoughs, handcrafted and baked the old fashioned way, on stone hearths. Also you will find croissants, danish pastries, lavosh, focaccias as well as fine cheese and wine.

Artisan Bread Company can be found at 11300 Lindbergh Blvd, in Ft. Myers, FL (just east of I-75, off Daniels Pkwy.) Any bread lover will be glad they made the trip!

sauces & sides

Clarified Butter

Clarified butter is a clear yellow liquid that is used primarily for sautéing delicate foods, such as fish filets and anything that is breaded. All of the impurities that cause butter to burn so quickly at low temperatures, have been removed. Since it takes just as much time to make a small quantity as it does a large batch, make enough so that you can use it regularly.

1 lb. unsalted butter

In a heavy saucepan, such as enamel-lined cast-iron, melt the butter over low heat and soon as butter is melted and very foamy, about 10 minutes, remove the pan from heat and carefully skim off all of the foam that has risen to the surface and discard. The strained, clear yellow liquid is clarified butter and can be stored in a tightly covered jar in the refrigerator for up to 3 weeks or can be frozen for 2 to 3 months. You can use clarified butter for sautéing in any recipe that calls for regular butter.

MAKES ABOUT 6 TO 8 OUNCES

This recipe can easily be doubled or tripled.

Garlic Butter

Of the three garlic butters and oils we include in the book, this one is the most basic calling just for good quality unsalted butter and tons of fresh garlic. The uses are endless.

8 Tbs. (1 stick) salted butter

4 large garlic cloves, peeled and finely minced

Optional: 1 Tb. freshly squeezed lemon juice

In a small saucepan, melt the butter over low heat. Add the garlic and cook for 6 to 7 minutes or until just translucent. Add the optional lemon juice for a little tart flavor. Serve the garlic butter over crab cakes or drizzled over grilled fish, scallops or shrimp.

MAKES 1/2 CUP

Spicy Garlic and Herb Butter

This butter is so delicious tossed with steamed or grilled scallops or shrimp. You can also top your favorite grilled or pan-seared fish filets with a tablespoon or two for a burst of flavor.

1 lb. unsalted butter, softened

4 Tbs. finely minced fresh garlic

2 Tbs. finely minced fresh shallots

1 t. freshly squeezed lemon juice

1 t. kosher salt

½ t. freshly ground white pepper

1 t. Crystal hot sauce or other hot sauce

2 Tbs. roughly chopped fresh parsley

In the workbowl of a food processor, combine all of the ingredients except for the parsley and process until well blended. Add the parsley and pulse until just combined. Do not over process.

Transfer the herbed butter to a small bowl, cover and refrigerate until needed.

MAKES 1 POUND

Garlic, Onion and Ginger Oil

This flavorful oil is great for sautéing shellfish, fish filets and chicken. Also, if you decide to grill fish or meat on a whim and are pressed for time to marinate, brush the food with some of the oil just before placing them over the hot coals. Your grilled dish will then take on the wonderful aromas the oil has to offer.

1 qt. olive oil

4 whole garlic heads, peeled and cloves chopped

½ small onion, peeled and chopped

1 Tb. freshly grated ginger

In a medium sized saucepan, heat the oil over medium-low to low heat until just warm. Add the garlic, onion and ginger and simmer slowly for 30 minutes or until the oil becomes fragrant. Be careful not to burn the vegetables or the oil will taste bitter. Strain the oil into glass jars and let cool completely. Cover tightly and refrigerate until needed. Let the oil come back to room temperature about 30 minutes before using in the desired recipe.

MAKES 1 QUART

Lemon Beurre Blanc

With this basic recipe, you can create a variety of sauces. Try adding tiny capers, minced herbs and/or fresh garlic or spices such as curry powder for a more complex flavor. Lime juice works well with all fish dishes when substituted for the lemon juice and I also love whisking in a pureed roasted red pepper which takes the sauce to a very different level. Have fun experimenting!

1/2 cup freshly squeezed lemon juice

1/2 cup dry white wine

1/2 t. kosher salt

1/4 t. freshly ground white pepper

1/2 small bay leaf

1/2 cup heavy cream

2 cups (1 lb.) unsalted butter, cut into Tb. size pieces, and lightly chilled

In a heavy-bottomed 2 quart saucepan, combine the lemon juice, wine, salt, pepper and bay leaf. Cook over medium heat until the liquid has reduced by half.

Add the heavy cream, bring to a boil and again reduce by half. Remove and discard the bay leaf. Remove the saucepan from the heat and let the reduction cool slightly.

Reduce the heat to the lowest possible setting. Return the saucepan to the heat and start adding the butter 3 tablespoons at a time, whisking constantly and making sure that each portion of butter is absorbed before adding the next. The sauce should be smooth and creamy. Taste and correct the seasoning, cover and keep warm over barely lukewarm water until serving.

MAKES ABOUT 2 1/4 CUPS

Fresh Mango Beurre Blanc

1 Tb. unsalted butter

2 Tbs. finely minced onion

2 t. finely minced garlic

1 cup cubed fresh mango

1 recipe Lemon Beurre Blanc, see recipe above

Optional:
2 to 4 Tbs. dry white wine

Kosher salt and freshly ground white pepper

In a small skillet, melt the butter over medium-low heat. Add the onions, garlic and mango, cook for 2 to 3 minutes, stirring often, until the onions are soft but not browned.

Transfer the mango mixture to the container of a blender and pulse until smooth. With the machine running, pour the beurre blanc through the opening at top slowly, until all has been added and the mixture is very smooth. If the sauce is too thick, thin it out with a little of the optional white wine. Season with salt and pepper. Place the mixture in the top of a double boiler and set over lukewarm water until serving.

MAKES 3 1/2 CUPS

Pink Gulf Shrimp and Cream Cheese Spread

This darn spread is so addicting that if preparing it for a cocktail party, you better have made a ton, because it's going to disappear before you serve the first drink!

1 lb. unsalted butter, softened

12 oz. cream cheese

1 small onion,
peeled and finely minced

2 Tbs. finely minced garlic

2 Tbs. dry sherry

1 Tb. Gator Hot Sauce
or other hot sauce

1 Tb. kosher salt

$^{1}/_{2}$ t. freshly ground white pepper

1 Tb. freshly squeezed lemon juice

2 lbs. shrimp, preferably pink
Gulf shrimp, peeled, deveined
and cooked

GARNISH:

1$^{1}/_{2}$ Tbs. finely minced
fresh parsley

In the workbowl of a food processor, combine all of the ingredients except for the shrimp and process until thoroughly mixed. Add the shrimp and pulse to the desired consistency. The spread is equally delicious either smooth or chunky.

Transfer the spread to a crock or decorative serving bowl, sprinkle with the parsley and serve chilled with slices of French baguette or assorted crackers.

MAKES ABOUT 3 1/2 CUPS

Pan-Roasted Garlic and Lemon Aioli

Don't limit yourself to serving this garlicky sauce with only fish. It is so delicious served as a dip for steamed vegetables that you're never going to make that powdered onion soup mistake ever again.

4 Tbs. olive oil

14 large garlic cloves, peeled and coarsely chopped

2¼ cups mayonnaise

1 Tb. freshly squeezed lemon juice

½ t. Worcestershire sauce

½ t. Crystal hot sauce or other hot sauce

Kosher salt and freshly ground white pepper

1 Tb. finely minced fresh parsley

In a small skillet, heat the oil over medium-low heat. Add the garlic and cook, stirring often, until golden brown. Strain the garlic, discarding the oil and transfer the garlic to the container of a blender, together with all of the remaining ingredients except for the parsley, season with salt and pepper and blend again until very smooth.

Transfer the aioli to a serving bowl, sprinkle with the parsley and serve with grilled or fried fish.

MAKES ABOUT 2 1/2 CUPS

Sweet Pickle Relish Tartar Sauce

I just can't for the life of me understand why someone would buy that awful jarred excuse for a tartar sauce when making it from scratch couldn't be any easier. Make this recipe in quantity, you're going to spoon it on everything!

1¾ cups mayonnaise

½ cup sweet pickle relish

1 Tb. freshly squeezed lemon juice

¼ t. Worcestershire sauce

¼ t. onion powder

¼ t. dry mustard

Kosher salt and freshly ground white pepper

In a medium size mixing bowl, combine all of the ingredients and whisk until well blended. Season with salt and pepper, cover and refrigerate for at least 1 hour before serving so that the flavors can meld. Serve chilled with fried or grilled fish.

MAKES 2 CUPS

Creamy Mustard Sauce

This sauce goes so nicely with any grilled fish or meat. Whisk in about 2 to 3 tablespoons of horseradish and 1 tablespoon of grainy prepared mustard and use it as a dip for crispy home-made French fries or slather it on a warm corned beef sandwich.

2 Tbs. dry mustard

1 Tb. steak sauce

1 Tb. Worcestershire sauce

1 cup mayonnaise

½ cup heavy cream

Salt and freshly ground white pepper

Combine all of the ingredients in a small bowl and whisk until well blended. Season with salt and pepper to taste, cover and refrigerate 30 minutes before serving.

MAKES 1 1/2 CUPS

Randy's Mustard/Lemon Sauce for Crab Cakes

This sauce works well with other fried fish or shellfish but can also double as a perfect dressing for salads. Try this: fold in 3 tablespoons of minced parsley, ⅓ cup each of very finely diced red onion and red bell pepper, 1 large mashed garlic clove and 1 finely minced hard boiled egg. Toss with 3 lbs. of quartered and cooked small red potatoes and you'll have a winner of a salad for barbecues or picnics.

1 whole large egg

Juice from 1 large lemon

1 t. Dijon mustard

2 cups mayonnaise

1 t. Worcestershire sauce

1 t. Old Bay Seasoning

Salt and freshly ground black pepper

In a large mixing bowl, combine the egg, lemon juice, mustard, mayonnaise, Worcestershire and Old Bay and whisk until well blended. Season with salt and pepper to taste, cover and refrigerate until needed.

MAKES 2 1/4 CUP

If you prefer the sauce a little on the spicy side, add about 1 to 2 teaspoons of chili oil or other hot sauce and whisk well.

Randy's Brown Sauce

¼ cup canola oil

¼ cup all-purpose flour

2 cups Chicken Stock,
(see recipe page 75)

1 cup beef broth

1 t. dark brown sugar

1 t. oyster sauce

1 t. black bean sauce
(thick soy sauce)

Freshly ground white pepper

2 Tbs. water

2 Tbs. cornstarch

In a heavy 2 quart saucepan, heat the oil over medium heat. Add the flour and cook for 1 minute, stirring constantly or until the flour starts to brown. Add the chicken stock and beef broth and whisk until well blended.

Add the sugar, oyster sauce and bean sauce and season with pepper. Bring to a boil, reduce heat and simmer for 10 minutes, whisking often.

In a small bowl, whisk together the water and cornstarch. Add the mixture to the sauce, whisking constantly, until the sauce thickens. Remove from the heat, strain the sauce through a fine sieve and use in the desired recipe.

MAKES 1 QUART

Oyster sauce and black bean sauce are available in Oriental markets or the Asian section in your local supermarket.

"Ours is Better" Cocktail Sauce

I think the title speaks for itself. Need I say more?

*¹/₂ cup freshly grated
or jarred horseradish*

*1 Tb. Crystal Hot Sauce
or other hot sauce*

*1 Tb. Gator Hammock Sauce,
(see Resources page 200)*

3 Tbs. Worcestershire sauce

1 Tb. freshly squeezed lemon juice

1 cup chili sauce

1 cup Ketchup

Salt and freshly ground pepper

In a medium size bowl, combine all of the ingredients and whisk until well blended. Season with salt and pepper, cover and refrigerate for about 20 minutes before serving so that the flavors can meld. Serve lightly chilled with boiled, grilled or fried shellfish.

MAKES 2 1/2 CUPS

Marinara Sauce

This recipe makes a lot of sauce but since it is so versatile it's great to make ahead and freeze in plastic containers for future meals. Every well-stocked kitchen should always have a stash of good marinara sauce in the freezer for last minute menu planning!

4½ Tbs. olive oil

½ cup finely chopped onions

6 Tbs. finely minced fresh garlic

6½ lbs. canned, peeled plum tomatoes, including juices, crushed by hand

1 lb. fresh plum tomatoes, peeled, seeded and crushed by hand

¼ cup finely chopped fresh basil

2 Tbs. dried oregano

Salt and freshly ground black pepper

In a large stock pot, heat the oil over medium-low heat. Add the onions and garlic and cook, stirring often, for 10 minutes or until soft but not browned. Add the canned and fresh tomatoes, including juices, together with the basil and oregano, season generously with salt and pepper and simmer, partially covered, for 1 hour, stirring from time to time.

Remove from the heat and let cool completely. Fill plastic containers with the sauce, cover tightly and freeze for use in your favorite recipes or simply tossed with "al dente" pasta and a good grating of Parmesan cheese.

MAKES ABOUT 4 QUARTS

Randy's Seasoned Croutons

These delicious croutons make a terrific spicy topping for your favorite green or Caesar salad or a crunchy accompaniment to any of our soups, seafood stews or gumbo. Careful, they're so tasty that you might just eat them all before having a chance to serve them!

2 Tbs. granulated garlic

2 Tbs. granulated onion

$1/2$ oz. freshly ground black pepper

$1/4$ t. ground cumin

$1/4$ t. dry mustard

1 Tb. sweet paprika

1 Tb. kosher salt

2 Tbs. dried oregano

1 loaf French bread

2 to 4 Tbs. olive oil

Preheat oven to 375 degrees.

In a small mixing bowl combine all of the spices and herbs and mix well. Set aside.

Cut the French bread into $1/2$ inch cubes and place them in a large mixing bowl. Drizzle olive oil over the bread cubes and toss lightly to coat on all sides. Sprinkle with the seasoning mix and again toss to coat evenly.

Spread the cubes in a single layer on a baking sheet, place in the center of the preheated oven and bake for 6 to 8 minutes or until golden brown, turning the cubes with a spatula from time to time to brown evenly. Remove from the oven and let cool completely. Store in airtight containers.

SERVES 8 TO 10

Florida Avocado Guacamole

Any guacamole or "Indian Butter", (I love that name), relies solely on the quality of the avocados. We're fortunate enough to have our restaurant in Florida where our big, green, smooth-skinned avocados are readily available. If you have a difficult time finding them, you can always use the more common variety, the smaller Haas avocado, with it's almost black, bumpy coating. Either way make sure the avocado is ripe which should be a little soft to the touch when squeezed lightly, for best results.

2 large ripe Florida avocados, peeled and pitted

1 ripe medium tomato, seeded and diced

2 medium scallions, trimmed and finely chopped

2 large garlic cloves, peeled and finely minced

1 Tb. freshly squeezed lemon juice

1 jalapeño pepper, seeded and finely minced

1 t. kosher salt

1 t. freshly ground white pepper

In a medium mixing bowl, mash the avocado with a fork to a chunky consistency. Fold in the remaining ingredients and mix well. Cover and refrigerate for at least 20 minutes before serving. Taste and correct the seasoning and serve chilled with tortilla chips.

SERVES 8

Spiced Orange Marmalade Dipping Sauce

Not only is this sauce great for dipping but it also makes a fabulous glaze for grilled chicken or fish. Once you've removed the chicken or fish from the grill, brush it lightly while it's still warm, with some of the marmalade sauce. It will create a glossy, spicy blanket of flavor.

1 cup orange marmalade

¼ cup prepared horseradish

2 Tbs. Dijon mustard

2 Tbs. sour cream

1 Tb. finely minced Italian parsley

Kosher salt and freshly ground white pepper

In a medium mixing bowl, combine all of the ingredients and mix well. Season with salt and pepper and serve the sauce at room temperature or lightly chilled with our Coconut Crusted Shrimp (page 33) or any other fried seafood.

MAKES 1 1/2 CUPS

Roasted Tomato Salsa

Salsa number one, yep, number one of three salsas we include in the book. Why? Because who could have enough salsa recipes? We put salsa on almost everything from omelets to tortilla chips boosting the sales of jarred and fresh packed salsas to make them one of the most popular supermarket condiments in decades. They have become a kitchen staple with every pantry stocked of at least one, maybe two or even…three varieties!

6 large fresh ripe tomatoes, seeded and chopped

3 large garlic cloves, peeled and finely minced

2 Tbs. olive oil

1 medium onion, peeled and finely diced

1/2 medium green bell pepper, cored, seeded and finely diced

1/2 medium red bell pepper, cored, seeded and finely diced

2 jalapeño peppers, seeded and finely minced

1 Tb. finely minced fresh cilantro

1 Tb. freshly squeezed lemon juice

2 t. kosher salt

1 t. coarsely ground black pepper

Preheat the broiler.

Place the tomatoes on a baking sheet, sprinkle with the garlic and drizzle with the olive oil. Set under the broiler until lightly browned.

Transfer the tomato mixture to a medium mixing bowl. Add the remaining ingredients and mix well. Taste and correct the seasoning, cover and refrigerate for at least 45 minutes before serving. Serve with tortilla chips or with grilled fish.

SERVES 10 to 12

Fresh Tomato and Mango Salsa

Salsa number two is much less traditional with the addition of the sweet flavor of ripe mangoes. Did you know that mangoes, used extensively in tropical regions, are considered a vegetable when green and a fruit when ripe? So, here is a cooling fruit and vegetable salsa perfect to be served with grilled fish.

4 large ripe mangoes,
peeled and diced

3 large ripe tomatoes,
peeled, seeded and diced

2 Tbs. Randy's Key Lime Juice
or other lime juice

1 small onion,
peeled and finely diced

4 medium scallions,
finely minced, green part only

¹/₂ medium red bell pepper,
cored, seeded and finely diced

1 Tb. finely minced fresh cilantro

2 serrano peppers,
seeded and finely minced

1 Tb. kosher salt

1 t. freshly ground white pepper

2 Tbs. olive oil

In a large mixing bowl combine all of the ingredients and mix well. Cover and refrigerate for at least 30 minutes before serving. Serve as desired.

SERVES 12

Mango and Bell Pepper Salsa

When someone says "salsa", we usually think of the classic tomato-based, red table relish found all throughout Mexico…the Salsa Mexicana. But these days chefs are labeling almost any diced raw vegetable or fruit concoction that incorporates a few of the essential traditional seasonings such as cilantro, jalapeño peppers and onions a "salsa". Well, I'm guilty as well for such is our third and final recipe in this category. There's not a tomato to be found!

1 jalapeño pepper

4 ripe mangos, peeled and cubed

1 medium red bell pepper, cored, seeded and diced

1 medium green bell pepper, cored, seeded and diced

1/2 medium onion, peeled and diced

3 medium scallions, trimmed and diced

1/4 cup unsweetened pineapple juice

2 Tbs. white vinegar

1 t. kosher salt

1 t. freshly ground white pepper

2 Tbs. fresh cilantro, finely minced

2 Tbs. olive oil

Cut the jalapeño pepper in half. Remove the stem, seeds and membranes and discard. Finely dice the pepper and transfer to a medium size mixing bowl.

Add the remaining ingredients and mix well. Let stand at room temperature for 30 minutes. Cover and chill until serving.

MAKES ABOUT 1 QUART

Fresh Mango, Papaya and Pineapple Relish

Hold on! Isn't this a salsa or even more a chutney? Point taken. When you consider that the Indian word for "chutney" is derived from the word for "relish" and that "salsa" translates as "sauce", it's imperative that you realize labels are not the least bit important and all of the "little sides" in this section are basically variations on the same theme. So when in doubt, call it a relish, or a salsa or even a chutney which may not be exact but most likely you won't be wrong.

1 large fresh mango,
peeled and finely diced

1 fresh medium papaya,
peeled, seeded and finely diced

1 cup finely diced fresh pineapple

1 small onion,
peeled and finely diced

1/4 cup finely diced red bell pepper

1 Tb. finely minced fresh ginger

2 Tbs. finely minced fresh garlic

1 1/2 t. finely minced habanero pepper

1/2 cup red wine vinegar

1/2 cup apple cider vinegar

1/2 cup pineapple juice

1/4 cup granulated sugar

1 1/2 t. Chinese 5-spice powder

1/4 cup finely minced scallions,
green part only

Freshly ground white pepper

In a large saucepan, combine all of the ingredients, except for the scallions. Bring to a boil, reduce heat and simmer, uncovered, for 40 minutes, stirring often.

Remove the saucepan from the heat, add the scallions and season the relish with white pepper. Transfer to a medium size bowl and let cool. Cover and refrigerate. Serve the relish either warm or chilled.

SERVES 8

Warm Spiced Tropical Fruit Mojo

This sauce is so yummy you'll want to spoon it over everything! This "New World" combination of sweet fruit, spicy vegetables and pungent spices has a unique character, all its own. I especially love to serve it slightly warm and simply draped over pan-seared, grilled or roasted fish.

1/2 cup fresh crushed pineapple

1/2 cup fresh diced mango

1/2 cup fresh diced papaya

1 1/2 cups pineapple juice

1 t. finely minced habanero pepper

1 Tb. finely minced garlic

1 Tb. finely minced shallots

3 Tbs. red wine vinegar

1 t. kosher salt

1 t. coarsely ground black pepper

1/4 t. ground nutmeg

1/4 t. ground cinnamon

2 Tbs. water

2 Tbs. cornstarch

1 Tb. finely minced fresh cilantro

In the workbowl of a food processor, combine all of the ingredients except for the water, cornstarch and cilantro and process until smooth. Transfer the mixture to a 2 quart saucepan and simmer over medium to medium-low heat for 20 minutes; do not let the mixture come to a boil.

Combine the water and cornstarch in a small bowl and stir until the cornstarch has dissolved. Stir the mixture into the chutney and simmer for another 3 to 5 minutes or until the sauce has thickened. Remove the pan from the heat, add the cilantro and transfer the chutney to a serving bowl. Serve warm.

MAKES ABOUT 2 1/2 CUPS

Balsamic Vinaigrette

Balsamic vinegar, called Italian Black Gold, has become so popular here in the states that it has become the vinegar of choice when making a vinaigrette. There are so many Balsamic vinegars on the market ranging from five or six dollars to upwards as high as sixty dollars for one bottle. It all depends on the age of the vinegar; the longer it's aged, the more mellow and refined it will be. Spring for a reasonably priced good quality aged Balsamic vinegar such as Fini. Its mildly sweet and slightly acidic taste also makes it a perfect choice for serving as is, right from the bottle, drizzled lightly onto grilled fish or vegetables.

$\frac{1}{2}$ cup water

1 cup good quality balsamic vinegar

2 t. Dijon mustard

2 Tbs. freshly squeezed lemon juice

1 t. finely minced garlic

1 t. dried oregano

1 t. granulated sugar

1 t. chopped fresh parsley

1 cup extra-virgin olive oil

Salt and freshly ground black pepper

In the workbowl of a food processor, combine all of the ingredients except for the olive oil and process for 30 seconds. With the machine running, pour the oil very slowly through the feed tube until all of the oil has been added and vinaigrette is creamy. Season with salt and pepper to taste.

Cover and refrigerate the vinaigrette for at least 30 minutes. Bring the vinaigrette back to room temperature before serving.

SERVES 10 to 12

Double Raspberry Vinaigrette

$1\frac{1}{2}$ cups raspberry jam

$\frac{1}{2}$ cup raspberry vinegar

$\frac{3}{4}$ cup white vinegar

$\frac{1}{2}$ cup canola oil

1 t. kosher salt

1 t. coarsely cracked black pepper

Combine all of the ingredients in a medium size mixing bowl and whisk until well blended. Store in a tightly covered jar in the refrigerator. Shake well before using.

MAKES 3 1/4 CUPS

Randy's Blue Cheese Dressing

One of my favorite ways to serve this blue cheese dressing is atop a juicy and spicy hamburger. Shape fresh lean ground chuck into 6 ounce patties, sprinkle both sides with my Blackening Spice or any other good blackening seasoning and pan fry or grill to desired doneness. I prefer mine medium rare. Serve the burgers on our lightly toasted Sandwich Rolls (page 128) and top each with 2 tablespoons of blue cheese dressing, a fresh ripe slice of tomato and a generous portion sautéed red onions. Enjoy!

1/4 cup sour cream

3 Tbs. evaporated milk

1/2 t. granulated garlic

1/2 t. coarsely ground black pepper

1 Tb. white vinegar

1 cup mayonnaise

4 oz. (1/2 cup), blue cheese, crumbled

Optional: Kosher salt

In a medium size mixing bowl, combine the sour cream, milk, garlic, pepper, vinegar and mayonnaise and whisk until well blended. Fold in the blue cheese and season very lightly with salt if desired. Cover and refrigerate for at least 30 minutes before serving.

MAKES ABOUT 1 1/2 CUPS

10,000 Island Dressing

Why 10,000 and not just Thousand? Because we live in the land of the 10,000 Islands, from Naples south around the horn to Key West! Forgive me…I was just being cute!

1 cup mayonnaise

3/4 cup ketchup

2 Tbs. Worcestershire sauce

1 Tb. freshly squeezed lemon juice

1/2 cup sweet relish

1/4 cup dill pickle relish

1/4 cup chili sauce

Salt and freshly ground white pepper

In a medium mixing bowl, combine the mayonnaise, ketchup, lemon juice and Worcestershire sauce and whisk until well blended.

Fold in the relishes and chili sauce, season with salt and white pepper and blend well. Cover and refrigerate at least 1 hour before serving.

MAKES 2 3/4 CUPS

Creamy Coleslaw

This creamy coleslaw gets better and better the longer it sits in the refrigerator so plan on making it at least a day ahead of serving.

THE DRESSING:

2 cups mayonnaise

1 cup sour cream

1 Tb. Dijon mustard

3/4 cup red wine vinegar

1 t. kosher salt

1 t. freshly ground white pepper

1 cup granulated sugar

1 Tb. poppy seeds

1 Tb. celery seeds

1/2 t. hot sauce

THE SLAW:

2 1/2 cups shredded green cabbage

2 cups shredded red cabbage

1 medium onion, peeled and thinly sliced

2 medium carrots, peeled and shredded

3 scallions, trimmed and finely minced

Start by making the dressing: In a very large mixing bowl, combine the mayonnaise, sour cream, mustard, vinegar, salt, pepper, sugar, poppy seeds, celery seeds and hot sauce and whisk until well blended.

Add the cabbages, onion, carrots and scallions and fold until thoroughly combined with the dressing. Taste and correct the seasoning, cover and refrigerate until serving. Serve chilled.

SERVES 8

Macaroni and "Three" Cheese Casserole

This is one of those comfort food recipes that you just have to make two of: eat one right away and freeze one...if you can wait!

8 Tbs. unsalted butter

1½ Tbs. all-purpose flour

1 qt. half and half

1 lb. sharp or extra-sharp cheddar cheese, shredded

¼ lb. Asiago cheese, grated

¼ lb. Monterey Jack cheese, shredded

1 t. kosher salt

1 t. freshly ground white pepper

2 t. granulated garlic

2 Tbs. Worcestershire sauce

1 lb. macaroni, preferably small shells or elbows

TOPPING:

3 Tbs. unsalted butter

2½ cups Ritz crackers, crushed into crumbs

Preheat the oven to 350 degrees.

In a large heavy saucepan, melt the butter over medium-low heat. Add the flour and cook for 1 minute without browning, stirring constantly. Whisk in the half and half, bring to a simmer and cook for 4 to 5 minutes, whisking constantly. Add the cheeses and simmer, stirring constantly, until the cheeses have melted and the mixture is smooth and creamy. Season with the salt, pepper, garlic and Worcestershire sauce and reduce heat to very low. Keep warm.

Bring plenty of salted water to a boil in a large pot, add the macaroni and cook until barely tender, about 10 minutes. Drain well.

Remove the cheese sauce from the heat, fold in the cooked macaroni and mix well. Divide the mixture evenly among two, 2 quart casserole dishes. Set aside.

The topping: In a small skillet, melt the butter over medium-low heat. Add the cracker crumbs and cook for 1 to 2 minutes, stirring constantly, or until golden. Be careful not to burn. Sprinkle the crumbs evenly over the tops of each casserole, place them in the center of the preheated oven and bake for 20 to 30 minutes, or until bubbly and golden brown. Remove from the oven and serve one hot. Let the second one cool, cover and freeze to serve at a later time.

MAKES 2 CASSEROLES, ABOUT 8 SERVINGS

Red New Potato Salad with a Mustard Vinaigrette

I happen to have a passion for creamy potato salads over those that are tossed with a vinaigrette. Try substituting half of the mayonnaise for sour cream and add 3 ounces of smoky bacon, cooked until crisp and crumbled along with 3 tablespoons finely minced scallions to the finished salad for a delicious "baked potato" taste.

1/4 cup yellow mustard or Dijon mustard

1 cup mayonnaise

3 Tbs. freshly squeezed lemon juice

2 Tbs. red wine vinegar

1/2 cup finely minced red onion

Salt and freshly ground black pepper

2 lbs. small red new potatoes, skin on and quartered

In a large mixing bowl, combine the mustard, mayonnaise, lemon juice, vinegar and onion and whisk until well blended. Season with salt and pepper and set aside.

Bring salted water to a boil in a large pot, add the potatoes and cook until just tender, about 15 to 20 minutes. Drain well and let cool just about 10 minutes or until lukewarm.

Add the warm potatoes to the vinaigrette and fold gently but thoroughly. Taste and correct the seasoning, cover and refrigerate for at least 1 hour before serving. Serve chilled.

SERVES 4 TO 6

For a smoky taste, add 3 oz. of bacon, cooked until crisp and crumbled to the finished salad.

Island Rice Pilaf

This simple all-purpose side dish is a take on the Caribbean yellow rice pilaf. I like to use turmeric, known as "poor man's saffron", which basically creates a nice yellow color without imparting any specific flavor, making this pilaf a good foil for a lot of different spices and ingredients. So don't limit yourself to the exact recipe. Try adding cooked red beans or chick peas, diced tomatoes, steamed vegetables, poached shrimp, chipotle peppers or even a little curry powder. The possibilities are endless.

4 cups Chicken Stock, (see recipe page 75)

3 Tbs. finely diced red bell pepper

3 Tbs. finely diced green bell pepper

3 Tbs. finely minced red onion

3 Tbs. finely minced scallions

2 t. freshly ground white pepper

1 t. kosher salt

½ t. turmeric

2 cups converted white rice

In a 3 quart casserole, combine all of the ingredients except for the rice. Bring the mixture to a boil over medium-high heat and stir in the rice. Reduce the heat to low and simmer, covered, for 15 to 18 minutes or until the rice is just tender and all the liquid has been absorbed.

Remove the pan from the heat and let sit covered for 5 minutes. Fluff the rice with a fork and serve hot.

SERVES 6 TO 8

desserts

Brown Sugar Peanut Butter Cookies

I love this old-fashioned peanut butter cookie recipe the best because it makes a crisp, crunchy cookie with a lot of nutty flavor. Though dark brown sugar is called for, you can substitute light brown sugar but it's the amount of molasses in the dark variety that gives a more robust flavor… that which I prefer.

1 cup all-purpose flour, sifted

1/2 t. baking soda

1/4 t. salt

1/2 cup vegetable shortening

1/2 cup tightly packed dark brown sugar

1/2 cup granulated sugar

1 large egg

1/2 cup chunky peanut butter

1 Tb. water

1/2 t. pure vanilla extract

Preheat the oven to 325 degrees.

In a small bowl, sift together the flour, baking soda and salt and set aside.

In a medium mixing bowl, combine the shortening, sugars and egg and beat with an electric hand beater until well blended. Add the peanut butter, water and vanilla and continue to beat until smooth. Fold in the dry ingredients until thoroughly blended.

Prepare 2 cookie sheets by either greasing lightly or lining with parchment paper. Divide the cookie dough into 12 equal pieces and shape into balls. Place the dough on the prepared cookie sheets at least 2 inches apart on all sides. Dip a large fork in water and press the tines of the fork gently into the top of each ball, first in one direction and then in the other, to form a crisscross pattern and to flatten slightly.

Place the sheets in the center of the preheated oven and bake for 12 to 15 minutes or until golden brown. Transfer the cookies to wire racks to cool. Store the cookies in airtight containers for up to two weeks or you can freeze them successfully for up to 2 months.

MAKES 1 DOZEN

Grandmother Barzee's Chocolate Chip Cake with Brown Sugar Meringue

This recipe came from Randy's grandmother and then she gave it to my Grandmother and it's been in both of our families for over 60 years. We all request this cake for our birthdays. The cake has three layers, the first being a bottom layer that resembles a cookie dough texture. The next layer is chocolate chips and it is finally topped with a brown sugar meringue. Enjoy!

THE COOKIE DOUGH LAYER:

1 Tb. unsalted butter

2 cups all-purpose flour

¼ t. baking soda

1 t. baking powder

2 large egg yolks

¾ cup vegetable shortening

½ cup granulated sugar

1 t. pure vanilla extract

1 t. salt

1 Tb. water

THE SECOND LAYER:

1 bag (8 oz.) chocolate chips, any variety

THE MERINGUE TOPPING:

2 large egg whites

1 cup tightly packed light or dark brown sugar

Preheat the oven to 350 degrees. Using the butter, lightly coat the inside of a 9" square baking dish or cake pan and set aside.

Start by making the cookie dough layer: Sift together the flour, baking soda and baking powder into a medium size mixing bowl and reserve.

In a medium size mixing bowl combine the egg yolks, shortening, sugar, vanilla, salt and water and mix with a spatula until well blended. Gradually add the flour mixture and fold thoroughly; the dough will be quite crumbly. Transfer the mixture to the prepared baking dish and press with your fingers into a smooth even layer. Sprinkle the chocolate chips evenly over the dough and set aside.

The meringue topping: Place the egg whites in a stainless steel mixing bowl and with a hand held mixer, start to beat the egg whites on medium speed. As the whites begin to thicken, gradually add the brown sugar and continue beating until the meringue is shiny and forms stiff peaks, about 4 to 5 minutes.

Place the meringue over the chips but do not spread flat; keep it nice and fluffy with peaks. Place in the center of the preheated oven and bake for 40 minutes. Remove from the oven and let cool. To serve, cut into 9, 3 inch squares.

MAKES 9 (3 INCH) SQUARES

When making a meringue, never use a plastic bowl since the whites will never get fluffy and hold stiff peaks. Make sure the bowl is very clean; the tiniest bit of fat or grease will prevent the whites from beating. If using a copper bowl, which gives the most volume, make sure you rub the entire inside surface with the cut side of a lemon half This guarantees that there will not be a spec of fat or grease in the bowl.

Carrot Pineapple Cake with Vanilla Cream Cheese Icing

THE CAKE:

3 Tbs. unsalted butter, softened

1 1/2 cups shelled walnuts halves

2 1/3 cups all-purpose flour

3 1/2 t. ground cinnamon

1 t. ground ginger

2 1/2 t. baking powder

1/2 t. baking soda

1 t. salt

2 cups granulated sugar

1 cup canola oil

2 t. pure vanilla extract

4 large eggs

2 cups finely grated carrots

2 cans (8 oz. each) crushed pineapple, drained well

THE ICING:

3 packages (8 oz. each) cream cheese, softened

12 Tbs. (1 1/2 sticks) unsalted butter, softened

4 cups confectioner's sugar

2 t. pure vanilla extract

2 cups blanched sliced almonds

Start by making the cake: Preheat the oven to 350 degrees. Using the 3 tablespoons of butter, lightly coat the inside of three, 9" round cake pans, 1 1/2 inches high. Line the bottom of each with a round of parchment paper, butter the parchment paper and set aside.

In the workbowl of a food processor, combine the walnuts with 1/3 cup of the flour and process until the nuts are finely ground. Transfer the chopped nuts to a medium size mixing bowl and whisk in the remaining flour together with the cinnamon, ginger, baking powder, baking soda and salt. Reserve.

Combine the sugar, oil and vanilla in the bowl of an electric mixer and beat on medium speed until well blended. With the machine running, add the eggs one at a time, beating well after each addition. Reduce the speed to low, add the flour mixture and beat until the flour just disappears. With a large spatula, fold in first the nuts, then the carrots and pineapple, gently but thoroughly.

Divide the batter evenly among the 3 cake pans. Place in the center of the preheated oven and bake for 30 minutes or until a toothpick when inserted comes out clean. Remove the pans from the oven and place on wire racks to cool for 1 hour. Run knife around the inside edge of each pan and unmold onto wire racks. Set aside while making the icing.

The Icing: In a large bowl, combine the softened cream cheese and butter and beat with an electric hand mixer until smooth. Add the confectioner's sugar and vanilla and continue beating until well blended. Cover and chill the icing for at least 30 minutes or until firm enough to spread.

When the cakes have cooled, place one cake, bottom side up on a cake plate. Spread evenly, 3/4 cup of the icing over just the top of the cake. Top evenly with a second cake, bottom side up, pressing lightly so that the cake sticks to the icing. Spread evenly, another 3/4 cup of the icing on the cake and then top evenly with the third cake, top side up and again press lightly.

Spread about $^1/_3$ of the remaining icing over the top and sides of the cake and chill both the cake and the remaining icing for 30 minutes.

Spread again the top and sides of the cake with the remaining icing. With your hands, press the almonds to sides of the cake. Cut the cake with a slightly wet knife into wedges and serve lightly chilled.

SERVES 10 to 12

Creamy Cuban Flan

This flan recipe has its origin in the Caribbean and is quite different from the Mexican or Spanish version since it has a denser, richer flavor and an oh-so velvety texture.

THE CUSTARD:

8 oz. cream cheese, softened

1 can (12 oz.) evaporated milk

1 can (14 oz.) sweetened condensed milk

4 large eggs

1 t. pure vanilla extract

THE CARAMEL:

1 cup granulated sugar

1/4 cup water

In the container of a blender, combine the cream cheese, evaporated and condensed milk, eggs and vanilla and blend on medium speed until completely smooth. Set aside.

Preheat the oven to 350 degrees.

In a small heavy saucepan combine the sugar and water, bring to a boil over medium heat and stir once to dissolve the sugar. Continue to cook, without stirring, until the mixture turns a hazelnut brown; be careful not to burn. Immediately pour the mixture into the bottom of a round porcelain or glass baking dish or cake pan, 8 to 10" in diameter and at least $2^1/_2$ to 3" deep and quickly tilt and turn the dish so that the caramel covers the bottom evenly.

Pour the blended custard mixture into the baking dish and set the dish inside a larger baking pan. Fill the larger baking pan with boiling water to come halfway up the sides of the custard dish. Cover the pan with parchment paper or foil and place in the center of the preheated oven. Bake for 1 hour or until the custard is just set; the center of the flan should still *jiggle* a bit.

Remove the pan from the oven and remove the baking dish from the outer pan. Let cool completely and refrigerate overnight for best results which will make for a thick and creamy flan.

The next day, remove the flan from the refrigerator and run a warm knife around the inside edge of the dish to loosen. Place a large round deep platter upside down over the baking dish and carefully invert holding both the plate and pan together until the flan is released. Carefully lift the baking dish, allowing the caramel sauce to run down the custard and serve the flan chilled, sliced into wedges with some of the sauce.

SERVES 8

You may substitute an 8 ounce can of Coco Lopez for the cream cheese which will give a wonderful "coconut" flavor to the flan. Add it to the blender with the other ingredients.

Frannie's Truck Stop Rice Pudding

When I was dating Georgi back in High School, I would periodically make a detour to this one truck stop on the way home that served what I considered the BEST rice pudding ever. It was so creamy, delicious and comforting that I must confess, I stopped there quite a lot Georgi! Years went by and I had yet to find another pudding comparable; that is, until I opened the restaurant in Naples. I was telling my rice pudding slash love story to Frannie, one of our terrific servers and she said that she had a great recipe. So I asked her to make some for me and sure enough, one taste of this incredible pudding took me right back to the good old days. Thanks Frannie for the memories and resurrecting my long lost favorite rice pudding recipe!

1 Tb. unsalted butter

2/3 cup water

1/3 cup converted white rice

1 qt. warm whole milk

1/4 cup granulated sugar

1/4 t. kosher salt

4 large eggs

1 t. pure vanilla extract

Optional: 1/2 cup golden raisins

Preheat the oven to 300 degrees. Using the butter, lightly coat the inside of a 9" square glass baking dish.

In a small saucepan, bring water to a boil. Add the rice, reduce the heat to low and simmer, covered, for 15 to 18 minutes or until the rice is tender and all the water has been absorbed. Remove from the heat and let sit covered for 5 minutes. Reserve.

In another small saucepan, warm the milk over low heat. Remove the pan from the heat, add the sugar and stir until dissolved. Set aside.

Combine the eggs and vanilla extract and whisk until well blended. Whisk in the warm milk. Fluff the rice with a fork, fold it into the custard together with the optional raisins. Transfer the mixture to the prepared baking dish, place in the center of the preheated oven and bake for 50 to 60 minutes or until a toothpick when inserted comes out clean. Remove the dish from the oven, let cool slightly and serve warm or slightly chilled.

SERVES 4 to 6

Three Layer Peanut Butter Fudge Brownies

Pete, our baker extraordinaire, usually makes his delectable brownies for the restaurant in a super large baking pan and in triple the quantity but he cut back on ingredients and then painstakingly reworked and retested the recipe so that you can easily duplicate it at home. Thanks Pete, it works perfectly!

THE BROWNIE LAYER:

1½ cups plus 2 Tbs. unsalted butter, softened

2¼ cups all-purpose flour

1¼ cups unsweetened cocoa

1½ t. baking powder

½ t. salt

6 large eggs

3 cups granulated sugar

1½ t. pure vanilla extract

1½ cups peanut butter chips

THE PEANUT BUTTER LAYER:

½ cup unsalted butter, softened

½ cup granulated sugar

1½ cups creamy peanut butter

1 t. pure vanilla extract

3 Tbs. all-purpose flour

THE FUDGE FROSTING:

3 oz. unsweetened chocolate

1½ Tbs. water

4½ Tbs. unsalted butter, softened

¼ t. salt

1 t. pure vanilla extract

2 to 4 Tbs. confectioner's sugar

Start by making the brownie layer: Preheat the oven to 350 degrees. Using the 2 tablespoons of butter, lightly coat the inside of a baking dish measuring 9" x 13" x 2" deep or 10" x 12" x 2" deep and set aside.

Combine the flour, cocoa, baking powder and salt in a large mixing bowl and reserve.

In a large mixing bowl, whisk the eggs until well blended. Add the sugar and vanilla and whisk until thoroughly combined. Add the softened butter and continue whisking until the mixture is smooth and well blended. Whisk in the flour mixture until it just disappears. Fold in the peanut butter chips and transfer the batter to the prepared pan. Spread evenly with a spatula and set aside.

The peanut butter layer: Combine the butter and sugar in another large mixing bowl and whisk until well blended. Add the peanut butter and vanilla and continue whisking until smooth. Whisk in the flour until it just disappears. Drop the peanut butter batter by spoonfuls over the chocolate layer and spread evenly, being careful not to disturb the chocolate layer.

Place the baking dish in the center of the preheated oven and bake for 30 to 35 minutes or until a toothpick when inserted comes out clean. Remove from the oven and transfer to a wire rack to cool completely.

In the meantime, prepare the fudge frosting: In the top of a double boiler over simmering water, melt the chocolate together with the water until completely smooth. Remove the top of the boiler from the water, and set aside until the chocolate is lukewarm to the touch. Add the butter, salt, vanilla and 2 tablespoons of the confectioner's sugar and stir until very smooth. Taste the frosting and if you prefer it a little sweeter, add the remaining sugar. Spread the frosting evenly over the cooled brownie mixture with a cake spatula. Cut into squares and serve at room temperature or lightly chilled.

SERVES 10 to 12

Triple Chocolate Bread Pudding

Although I like to serve the pudding the same day, it can be made successfully 2 to 3 days in advance. Before serving, cover and place it in a 300 degree oven for about 10 to 15 minutes to make sure that it is nice and warm.

1 qt. heavy cream

4 cups semi-sweet chocolate chips

³/₄ cup granulated sugar

³/₄ cup light brown sugar

5 large eggs

2¹/₂ cups whole milk

18 cups cubed crusty bread, preferably Italian or French

2 Tbs. unsalted butter

GARNISH:

Fresh whipped cream or good quality vanilla ice cream

Chocolate syrup

In a heavy 2 quart saucepan, bring the heavy cream to a low simmer. Add 2 cups of the chocolate chips together with granulated sugar and brown sugar and stir constantly until the chocolate and sugars have completely melted and mixture is smooth. Reserve. You can also do this in the microwave: place the cream, chocolate and sugars in a large glass bowl, partially cover and microwave on high heat for 5 minutes or until the chocolate and sugars have melted.

Combine the eggs and milk in a very large mixing bowl and whisk until well blended. Add the warm chocolate cream and whisk until the custard is smooth. Add the bread cubes and toss well. Cover and set aside at room temperature for 1 hour or until the bread is completely soaked with the custard. Since the bread will float to the surface, spoon some of the custard over the cubes every 10 minutes with a large spoon making sure that they are completely immersed.

Preheat the oven to 350 degrees. Using the 2 tablespoons of butter, lightly coat the inside of a 9" x 13" x 2" baking dish or pudding dish.

Spoon half of the bread custard in the baking dish, sprinkle with the remaining chocolate chips and then top with the remaining bread custard. Set the baking dish inside a larger baking dish.

Place in the center of the preheated oven and fill the larger baking dish with boiling water so that it comes half way up the sides of the smaller baking dish. Bake for about 1 hour or until the custard is just set: a toothpick when inserted should come out clean. Remove the smaller baking dish from the oven and from the larger baking dish, uncover and let cool on a cake rack to room temperature.

Cut the pudding into squares and place on individual dessert plates. Top each portion with a dollop of whipped cream or a good quality vanilla ice cream, drizzle with a little chocolate syrup and serve at once.

SERVES 10 to 12

Chunky Peanut Butter Pie

This Southern favorite is not only easy, quick and economical to prepare, but equally delicious and the best part… it freezes beautifully.

2 packages (8 oz. each) cream cheese, softened at room temperature

1¼ cups chunky peanut butter

1 cup confectioner's sugar

3 cups Cool Whip, defrosted

3 ready-made (9 inches each) chocolate cookie crumb pie shells

OPTIONAL GARNISH:

Fresh whipped cream

Chocolate syrup

Chocolate curls (see remarks)

To the bowl of an electric mixer fitted with the paddle attachment, combine the cream cheese, peanut butter and sugar and beat on medium speed until very smooth. Remove the paddle, add the Cool Whip and fold gently but thoroughly.

Divide the mixture evenly among the 3 ready-made pie shells and refrigerate for at least 2 hours before serving.

When ready to serve, cut the pies in wedges and transfer to individual dessert plates. Simply serve chilled or top each portion with a dollop of whipped cream, a drizzle of chocolate sauce and a sprinkling of chocolate curls.

MAKES 3 (9-INCH) PIES

To make chocolate curls, you will need a 1 pound block of chocolate or a very thick bar. The chocolate must be at room temperature, and simply pull and drag a vegetable peeler over the edge of the chocolate to create curls. Store in airtight containers in the refrigerator until needed.

Dark Chocolate Double Espresso Cake

If you are unable to make espresso coffee, you can simply substitute 1 cup of regular prepared coffee mixed with 3 tablespoons of instant espresso coffee in the cake preparation and 3 tablespoons regular coffee mixed with 1 teaspoon instant espresso in the glaze.

THE CAKE:

1 lb. (4 sticks) unsalted butter

1 cup prepared espresso coffee

1 cup dark brown sugar

14 oz. good quality bittersweet chocolate, broken into pieces

8 large eggs

THE GLAZE:

12 oz. good quality bittersweet chocolate

12 Tbs. unsalted butter

3 1/2 Tbs. prepared espresso coffee

GARNISH:

Fresh whipped cream

Fresh raspberries

Start by making the cake: Preheat the oven to 350 degrees. Lightly coat the inside of a 9" round springform pan with a little of the butter. Line the bottom of the pan with a circle of parchment paper and butter the parchment. Set the pan aside.

In a heavy 2 1/2 quart saucepan, melt the butter together with the coffee and sugar over low heat and stir until the sugar is melted. Add the chocolate and stir until the chocolate is melted and mixture is completely smooth. Remove the pan from the heat and let the chocolate mixture cool to lukewarm. Whisk in the eggs, one at a time, until well blended.

Pour the batter into the prepared springform pan and set it inside a large baking dish. Place the dish in the center of the preheated oven and fill the baking dish with boiling water so that it comes half way up the sides of the springform pan. Bake for 1 hour.

When the cake is done, remove it from the oven and from the baking dish and transfer to a cake rack. Run a knife around the inside edge of the springform pan to loosen the cake and let cool to room temperature in the pan. Cover and refrigerate overnight.

The next day, loosen and remove the sides of the springform pan. Place a round serving platter upside down over the cake and carefully invert the cake onto the platter holding both the platter and cake together. The bottom of the cake will become the top. Remove the springform pan bottom and carefully peel off and discard the parchment paper. Set aside.

Prepare the glaze: In the top of a double boiler, combine the chocolate, butter and coffee, set over simmering water and stir until the chocolate has melted and the mixture is very smooth. Pour the warm glaze over the top of the cake to cover completely, letting it drip down and coat the sides of the cake. With a spatula, quickly touch up any of the uncoated areas on the sides of the cake.

Cut the cake with a slightly wet knife into wedges. Serve at room temperature or lightly chilled with a dollop of whipped cream and some fresh raspberries.

SERVES 12

Georgi's Sweet and Tart Key Lime Cake

My wife's Key Lime Cake is one of my favorites since it has a nice balance of sweet and tart and is so very moist. Georgi serves it as you would a pound cake, cut into slices and accompanied by a dollop of lightly sweetened whipped cream or good quality vanilla ice cream. Heaven!

THE CAKE:

1 Tb. unsalted butter

1 1/2 cups all-purpose flour

1 t. baking powder

1/2 t. salt

1 cup granulated sugar

1/2 cup canola oil

2 large eggs

2 Tbs. finely grated lime zest

1/2 cup whole milk

THE SIMPLE SYRUP:

1/2 cup Randy's Key Lime Juice or other bottled lime juice

1/2 cup granulated sugar

Start by making the cake: Preheat the oven to 350 degrees. Using the butter, lightly coat the inside of a standard, 1 pound loaf pan (8 1/4" x 4 1/4" x 2 1/2") and set aside.

In a medium mixing bowl, sift together the flour, baking powder and salt and reserve.

Combine the sugar, oil, eggs, zest and milk in a large bowl and whisk until pale yellow. Add the reserved dry ingredients and whisk until the flour mixture just disappears. Pour the batter into the prepared loaf pan and set in the center of the preheated oven. Bake for 40 to 50 minutes or until a toothpick when inserted comes out clean.

Remove the cake from the oven, place on a wire cake rack and let cool in the loaf pan.

While cake is cooling, prepare the simple syrup: In a small saucepan, combine the sugar and lime juice. Place over medium heat, bring to a boil and stir to dissolve the sugar. Remove from the heat and cool completely.

When the cake has cooled, brush the entire simple syrup over the top to give the cake a nice tart finish and let sit until all of the syrup is absorbed. To serve, remove the cake from the pan and cut into 1/2 inch slices.

MAKES 1 (1 POUND) LOAF

When we photographed our lime cake for this cookbook, we garnished with fresh raspberries and drizzled the sliced cake with a little lime/sugar glaze. To make the glaze, combine 1/4 cup confectioner's sugar with 1 tablespoon lime juice and whisk until smooth. Add more juice, drop by drop, to achieve the desired consistency.

Randy's Famous Key Lime Pie

I had been making my simple yet delicious Key Lime Pie for more than 15 years in Southwest Florida before I was "discovered" by QVC. The Pie was such a huge success on this home shopping channel, with orders through the roof that I needed to build a separate factory solely for producing these pies! Enjoy!

1 can (14 oz.) sweetened condensed milk

6 oz. Cool Whip, defrosted

4 oz. Randy's Famous Key Lime Juice or other lime juice

1 ready made (9-inch) graham cracker pie crust

GARNISH:

Lightly sweetened whipped cream

In the bowl of an electric mixer, combine the condensed milk with the Cool Whip and beat on low speed for 10 minutes.

Add the lime juice to the mixer and beat on low speed for 10 minutes longer. Pour the pie filling into the prepared crust and refrigerate for at least 3 hours or overnight. Serve the pie cut into wedges and topped with a dollop of whipped cream.

MAKES 1 (9-INCH) PIES

On a warm summer evening, this pie is equally delicious served frozen.

"No Hassle" Key Lime Cheesecake

No hassle is exactly right! A couple of ingredients mixed together all in one bowl, spooned into a cracker crust and set in the refrigerator without baking. You could swear that this super light and fluffy cheesecake took hours to prepare.

2 packages (8 oz. each) cream cheese, softened

2 cans (14 oz. each) sweetened condensed milk

1/2 cup Randy's Key Lime Juice or other lime juice

1 1/2 t. pure vanilla extract

2 t. very finely grated lime zest

2 ready made (9-inch) graham cracker pie crusts

In the bowl of an electric mixer, combine the cream cheese and condensed milk and beat until well blended. Add half of the lime juice, vanilla and zest and beat well. Add the remaining juice, vanilla and zest and beat until thoroughly incorporated.

Divide the mixture evenly between the two prepared pie crusts and refrigerate 6 hours or overnight. Serve chilled cut into wedges with a dollop of lightly sweetened whipped cream.

MAKES 2 (9 INCH) PIES

Flourless Chocolate Cake

Flourless chocolate cakes are the ingenious combination of the traditional chocolate mousse and the soufflé. The chocolate/egg mixture, the mousse is then baked like the soufflé but instead of being runny in the center, the cake is cooked all the way through. If you're a chocolate lover and like a deep rich taste, dust the finished cake with unsweetened cocoa instead of the confectioner's sugar.

16 Tbs. (2 sticks) unsalted butter plus 1 Tb.

8 oz. semi-sweet chocolate chips

1½ cup granulated sugar

1 cup unsweetened cocoa

6 large eggs

GARNISH:

Confectioner's sugar

Optional: 1 pint fresh raspberries

2 cups fresh whipped cream

Preheat the oven to 350 degrees. Butter the bottom and sides of a round 10" springform pan with the tablespoon of butter. Line the bottom of the pan with a circle of parchment or wax paper and then butter the paper. Set aside.

In a small heavy saucepan, combine the 16 tablespoons of butter and the chocolate chips. Place the pan over low heat and stir constantly until the chocolate and butter have melted and mixture is smooth. Remove from the heat and reserve.

Place the granulated sugar, cocoa and eggs in a large mixing bowl and whisk until well blended. Add the chocolate/butter mixture and fold gently but thoroughly. Pour the mixture evenly into the prepared pan.

Place the pan in the center of the preheated oven and bake for 35 to 40 minutes or until a toothpick when inserted comes out clean.

Remove the pan from the oven and let cool completely. Run a warm knife around the inside edge of the springform pan and loosen and remove the sides. Place a round serving platter upside down over the cake and carefully invert holding both the platter and cake together. The bottom of the cake will become the top. Remove the springform pan bottom and carefully peel off and discard the parchment paper. Dust the cake with confectioner's sugar and serve cut into wedges with the optional berries and whipped cream.

SERVES 8

Apple Crisp
with Brown Sugar Oatmeal Topping

A crisp, a crumble, a Brown Betty, they're basically all the same dish that have some combination of fruit, baked with a brown sugar/flour topping. We give a nice little twist to ours with the addition of rolled oats which makes for an extra crisp crust. Serve it nice and warm as is right from the baking dish or with a dollop of whipped cream or as we suggest in the recipe, a good scoop of vanilla ice cream.

6 Tbs. plus 2 t. unsalted butter

¾ cup dark brown sugar

½ cup all-purpose flour

½ cup old-fashioned rolled oats

¾ t. ground cinnamon

Pinch of freshly grated nutmeg

Optional: ½ cup chopped walnuts

4 cups peeled and sliced Golden,
Delicious or Macintosh apples

Preheat the oven to 350 degrees. Using the 2 tablespoons of butter, lightly coat the inside of a 9 inch square baking pan and set aside.

Combine the brown sugar, flour, oats, cinnamon, nutmeg, optional walnuts and the remaining butter in a medium size mixing bowl and reserve.

Add the apples to the prepared baking pan and sprinkle evenly with the brown sugar mixture. Place in the center of the preheated oven and bake for 30 to 35 minutes or until bubbly and golden brown. Remove the pan from the oven and let cool for 5 to 10 minutes before serving. Serve "a la mode" with a dollop of good quality vanilla ice cream.

SERVES 4

Tres Leches (Three Milk Cake)

For a more impressive presentation, you can instead spread the meringue completely and evenly over the entire surface of the cake and garnish with a mixture of fresh raspberries, blueberries, sliced strawberries and fresh mint leaves.

THE CAKE:

1 Tb. unsalted butter

2 cups all-purpose flour

4 t. baking powder

6 large eggs, separated

1/4 t. cream of tartar

2 cups granulated sugar

1/2 cup whole milk

THE TRES LECHES MILK:

1 cup half and half

1 can (12 oz.) evaporated milk

1 can (14 oz.) sweetened condensed milk

THE MERINGUE TOPPING:

1 cup light corn syrup

3 large egg whites

GARNISH:

1 pint fresh strawberries, hulled and sliced

Start by making the cake: Preheat the oven to 350 degrees. Using the butter, lightly coat the inside of a 9" x 13" x 2" deep baking dish and set side.

Sift the flour together with the baking powder in a small bowl and reserve. In the bowl of an electric mixer, combine the egg whites and cream of tartar and beat on medium speed until soft peaks form. With the mixer running, gradually add the sugar until the meringue is shiny and forms stiff peaks. Add the egg yolks, one at a time, beating thoroughly after each addition.

Reduce the speed to low and add the flour 1/2 cup at a time, until just mixed. Add the milk and beat until the mixture is just smooth; do not over mix. Pour the batter into the prepared pan and smooth evenly with a spatula. Place the pan in the center of the preheated oven and bake for 45 to 50 minutes or until a toothpick when inserted in the center of the cake comes out clean.

While the cake is baking, prepare the tres leches milk: In a large liquid measuring cup, combine the half and half, the evaporated milk and condensed milk and mix well.

When the cake is done, remove it from the oven, transfer to a wire cake rack and let cool for 10 minutes in the pan. Prick the top of the cake with a toothpick at 1 inch intervals and slowly pour all of the milk mixture over the top of the cake. Set the cake aside for 30 minutes or until it is completely cool and the milk has been absorbed. Cover the cake and refrigerate for at least 1 hour before serving.

The meringue: In a large stainless steel mixing bowl, combine the corn syrup and egg whites, set over just simmering water and beat with an electric mixer on high speed for 5 minutes. Remove the bowl from the heat and continue beating for 3 minutes longer or until completely cool. Cut the cake into squares and serve chilled with a dollop of the meringue and some sliced berries.

SERVES 12

RECIPE INDEX

Resources

Gator Hammock Sauces

800.664 2867

www.chilegator@msn.com

Baby's Coffee

Key West, Florida

800.523.2326

www.babyscoffee.com

Randy's Fishmarket Restaurant

239.593.5555

www.RandysFishmarketRestaurant.com

(Spices, Key Lime juice, shirts, mugs, and other fun stuff!)

To order this cookbook go to **info@randysfishmarketrestaurant.com**

or ask for it at your local bookstore.